THE Glories OF OUR Lord

THE Glories OF OUR Lord

H. C. HEWLETT

JOHN RITCHIE LTD.,
40 Beansburn, Kilmarnock, Scotland
GOSPEL FOLIO PRESS
P. O. Box 2041, Grand Rapids MI 49501-2041

A publication of
JOHN RITCHIE LIMITED
40 Beansburn, Kilmarnock, Scotland
and
GOSPEL FOLIO PRESS
P. O. Box 2041, Grand Rapids, Michigan

ISBN: John Ritchie 0-946351 41 4
Gospel Folio Press 1-882701-13-5

Typeset at Gospel Folio Press, Grand Rapids, Michigan
Printed by Bell and Bain Ltd., Glasgow

Foreword

Stand with me some summer night on an isolated hill and look up into the star-bejeweled heavens. The unaided eye can see about two thousand stars. Our sun, an average star, could contain 1,250,000 earths like ours. Yet some stars are large enough to swallow more than half our solar system! We wonder, with David, that their Maker would ever give a passing thought to the rebel sinners who inhabit the blue planet, third from the sun.

How *mighty* must He be who made the stars as "the work of [His] fingers" (Ps. 8:3). How *wise* must He be who knows the number of each one (Ps. 147:4). How *lofty* must He be who humbles Himself to "look on the things that are in heaven" (Ps. 113:6). Ah, but how *loving* must He be who came to this little orb and, on His way to the Cross, slept on just such a hillside with the stars as His only canopy.

This One is the focus of H. C. Hewlett's book. With what careful treatment and devotion the author deals with his Subject. Follow this wonderful journey from eternity through our Lord's Old Testament appearances, His Incarnation, Transfiguration, Crucifixion, and Exaltation. View in holy awe—if only from a distance—His Eternity, His Deity and Humanity. Learn more of the Son, the Great High Priest, and the Lamb. There is no grander subject. There is no greater occupation. May the Spirit make Him increasingly real to our hearts. As we open these pages, our prayer should be, "That I may know Him…" (Phil. 3:10).

J. B. NICHOLSON, JR.
GRAND RAPIDS, MICHIGAN

Contents

CHAPTER ONE

His Sonship

The higher mysteries of Thy fame
The creature's grasp transcend;
The Father only Thy blest Name
Of Son can comprehend. —J. Conder

In the inner life of God, apart from and before all created existence, is the infinite and holy fellowship of the three Persons of the Trinity. In this love-life is the joy of the Father in the Son, and of the Son in the Father, and both by the Holy Spirit. What Christ is to God in this relationship of love, and in its rich and abiding intimacy, is told out supremely in His name of Son. He bears many names and titles, as indeed all glories must meet on His brow. Certain of these tell what He is to creation, to His creatures, to His Church, or, it may be, to His land. But the name of Son tells what He is to God. His glory as Son is the source of all His relationships to His creatures, as it is the reason for all God's dealings in creation and in redemption. Therefore to consider the sonship of Christ is to consider the true key to the ways of God.

To begin, we must notice carefully the usage of the word "son" in the New Testament. Two words in particular are used on the original text, one referring to *dignity of position* and of character appropriate to this position, and the other to *relationship by birth*. While they are rendered "son" and "child" with little distinction in the Authorized Version, the Revised translates the first by "son," and the second by "child." Never is the second term spoken of the

Lord Jesus in His relationship to God, whereas believers are often so described. John in his writings does not use the first term for believers, except in Revelation 21:7, "He that overcometh shall inherit all things; and I will be his God, and he shall be My son." John reserves it for the Lord Jesus. Repeatedly John uses the second term for believers, for by the new birth they have become the Father's children. Paul frequently refers to them as the sons of God (using the first term), and in so doing emphasizes the high dignity of the fellowship with God into which they have been brought, rather than their possession of the divine life by the new birth.

Noting that "son" speaks of dignity, we think of our Lord's Sonship as stated in John 1:18, "No man hath seen God at any time; the only begotten Son, which is in the bosom of the Father, He hath declared Him." Notice the following truths we learn from this concerning the Son.

The uniqueness of our Lord's Sonship: He is the only begotten Son. Only begotten does not refer necessarily to birth, but to that which is unique in character and nature. This is seen in other uses of "only begotten" in the Scriptures. For example, "He that had received the promises offered up his only begotten son." Here Isaac's sonship linked with the promise sets him in a class alone, distinct from Ishmael and later sons of Abraham.

In addition to this passage in Hebrews 11, the term is used three more times in the New Testament other than of the Lord Jesus. In each of these it is translated "only." The son of the widow of Nain was the only son of his mother (Lk. 7:12); Jairus had an only daughter (Lk. 8:42); and the father of the afflicted lad called him "mine only child" (Lk. 9:38). In each case, the use of "only" emphasized not birth but the solitary character of the relationship, and hence its peculiarly dear nature to the parent.

When used of the Lord Jesus, *only begotten* sets forth the uniqueness and endearment of His relationship Godward. Of necessity He is alone in this glory. No one else can share it. This is exhibited in the words of Christ: "I ascend unto My Father, and your Father" (Jn. 20:17). He always speaks of "My" Father, never using "our" to include Himself. Those who have believed are partakers of the divine nature through grace as sons; Christ is Son as possessing Deity. This uniqueness is further declared in the word "own." The Jews sought to kill the Lord Jesus because He called God His *own* Father (Jn. 5:18, R.V.), and God spared not "His own Son" (Rom. 8:32).

The equality with God implied in the Sonship: Son is an expression of dignity, not of subjection, and still less of inferiority. There certainly is order in the Trinity, for the Father sent the Son and not the Son the Father, but this implies neither superiority nor inferiority. The fact that our Lord took the place of subjection to God in incarnation does not denote lesser value for the name "Son." Rather it shows the greatness of His humility. "*Though* He were a Son, yet learned He obedience by the things which He suffered" (Heb. 5:8). This clearly implies that His early path of suffering was set in contrast to His nature and glory as Son. Even the Jews realized His assertion of Sonship to be one of equality with God (Jn. 5:18). Admittedly, the term "son" had been applied by God to the people of Israel as a whole, but it was national in its significance. Personal sonship of God was never known until set forth in Christ Himself.

Our Lord's teaching in John 5:19-29 expressly claims for the Son a knowledge and power equal to the knowledge and power of the Father. It shows that "all men should honour the Son even as they honour the Father." While it is true that "the Son can do nothing of Himself," this is not because of any inferiority in Him; it is because of His place in the unity of the Godhead.

The Intimacy of His Sonship: The Son dwells in the bosom of the Father. It is the sphere proper to Him by virtue of His place in Deity. The expression "in the bosom" is used in Scripture of the relationships of close friends, of parents and children, and of husband and wife. Thus it indicates nearness and deep attachment. The phrase in John 1:18 is not strictly "in the bosom," but "into the bosom," speaking not only of place, but also of direction. It tells of the communion between Father and Son wherein all the Father's thoughts are reciprocated perfectly by the Son. It tells of One who "rests with face turned inwards," enjoying the fullness of the Father's love. There is no veil, no limited access, no measured intimacy, but the fullness of perfect knowledge and perfect joy.

This is the place John gives the Lord in the first chapter of his Gospel. But in his last chapter, he tells us that if the things which Jesus did should all be written, he supposes that even the world itself could not contain the books which should be written. Is not the lesson clear that only the bosom of the Father could contain Him? Only there could He be fully known and fully appreciated.

The eternity of His Sonship: Our Lord's Sonship is not a result of the incarnation. The relationships of Father and Son are intrinsic to the Godhead, and are the basis of revelation. In John 1:14, we read of "glory as of the only begotten from beside the Father." He had been beside the Father before He became flesh. In John 16:28, He says, "I came forth from the Father, and am come into the world; again, I leave the world, and go unto the Father." His being with the Father preceded His coming into the world, as His leaving the world preceded His going to the Father. In John 1:18, the expression "which is in the bosom" employs the present participle in its timeless sense, indicating not time but nature. It is the Son's nature to be in the bosom. It has been well said that "Christ came forth from the Father's bosom without ever leaving it."

If, in spite of these Scriptures, it is contended that the relationships of Father and of Son are linked only with Christ's manifestation in time, we ask what it was in the eternal relationship of the divine Persons that issued in that relationship of Father and Son in time? That there is order in the Trinity we have already seen, and this indicates a necessary relationship beyond time. Moreover, the relationships of Father and of Son are for the ages to come, and hence must have their spring in relationships that could be satisfied in no other fashion. Surely those that preceded the incarnation were not less sublime nor less precious than those which followed it. They must have possessed all the wealth of intimacy and love that was manifested by the Jordan and on the Holy Mount. We conclude that Scripture clearly teaches that Christ's Sonship is eternal.

The love that is essential in His Sonship: The bosom is love's abode where the Son dwells in the ceaseless embrace of eternal love. It is noteworthy that the first mention of love in Scripture is found in the words to Abraham in Genesis 22: "Take now thy son, thine only son Isaac, whom thou lovest." Here is the signpost to the study of love in the Word, the love of a father for his only begotten son. Later, in the Song of the Beloved in Isaiah 5, we find that the Lord of Hosts speaks of One whom He calls His well beloved, and to whom He attributes the bringing of Israel into their land. In the light of the parable of the vineyard— "having yet therefore one son, his well beloved" (Mk. 12:6)—the meaning is clear. Before the incarnation, our Lord was the well-beloved of God. This was His joy.

It is in the Gospel of John that the wealth of this love is

firmly set forth. Seven times there we are told of the love of the Father toward the Son:

"The Father loveth the Son, and hath given all things into His hand" (3:35). The Father's love is the fount which gives all things to the Son. These "all things" are the tribute of love that would lavish its fullness on its object, that finds in Him complete worthiness to possess all.

"The Father loveth the Son and showeth Him all things that Himself doeth" (5:20). Such is the warmth of this love that it can have no reserves of knowledge. All the deep counsels of the Father are spread openly before the Son.

"Therefore doth My Father love Me, because I lay down My life, that I might take it again" (10:17). The grace, the moral beauty displayed by the Son in His sacrificial obedience draws forth the Father's love, a love which manifests itself in giving to the Cross its triumphant sequels.

"As the Father hath loved Me, so have I loved you" (15:9). Here is the measure of the love of Christ to His people. As the Father has loved Him, with a love eternal—infinite and holy—so has the Son loved them. Can our hearts really take this in?

"I in them, and Thou in Me, that they may be made perfect in one; and that the world may know that Thou hast sent Me, and hast loved them, as Thou hast loved Me" (17:23). The Father's love to the Son is the same love that has embraced us in the Beloved. The greater we see the bliss of Christ as Son, the greater is our blessing in Him.

"Father, I will that they also, whom Thou hast given Me, be with Me where I am; that they may behold My glory, which Thou has given Me: for Thou lovedst Me before the foundation of the world" (17:24). This majestic verse embraces two eternities, and shows that the source of all our blessing, and of all Christ's joy in the ages to come, is the Father's love to Him in the past of eternity.

"That the love wherewith Thou hast loved Me may be in them, and I in them" (17:26). The love of the Father to the Son is to be our true portion and our ceaseless enjoyment as we ponder its eternal wealth and the vastness of its purposes of blessing.

The revelation of God resulting from His Sonship: No one else can so tell forth the Father as the One who knows all that there is in His bosom. From the depths of an intimacy without reserve, from its purity of light and love, and from the fulness of its life, the Son has come that we might know God. Need we wonder, then, that the expression "the bosom of the Father" is followed in a golden chain by four others like it, making another of those harmonies of thought so much a trait of John's writings.

First there is the bosom—the place of access, communion, and endearment. Then there is the Name—the index of character. There is the Will—which speaks of wise and holy purposes. There is the Hand, the sphere of power. Lastly there is the House—the place of ultimate rest.

"I am come in My Father's name," said Christ (5:43). He fully manifested the Father's character, vindicating its authority, and glorifying it by all that He was and said.

"This is the Father's will which hath sent Me, that of all which He has given Me I should lose nothing" (6:39). In doing that blessed will, the Son found His strength and refreshment. It was His food; to Him it was good and acceptable and perfect, and He rejoiced in the certainty of its blessing those who were His Father's gift to Him.

"No man is able to pluck them out of My Father's hand" (10:29). With His last words on the Cross, the Lord commended His Spirit into the Father's hands. He brings His own to security like this. There His sheep are cared for by final and absolute power.

"In My Father's house are many mansions" (14:2).

Heaven is a country, the land of our citizenship; a paradise, the place of fruitfulness; and a house, the sphere of family ties. There was no place for Him in the inn at the city of His father, David. But now He has ascended on high that by His acceptance in glorified manhood He may give us a place in the house of the Eternal Father. He came from the bosom that He might be the way to the house—indeed, the way to the Father, that in Him we might be embraced in His love as well. How complete is His revelation of the Father, both in itself and in its results for the redeemed.

So precious to God is the Sonship of Christ that He is pleased to give to it a threefold vindication. Proud men of earth may lift up their standard of rebellion against the God of heaven and deride the claims of His beloved Son, but He delights to acknowledge Him and to proclaim His worth. Beside the Jordan and on the Mount of Transfiguration, God speaks from the opened heaven: "This is My beloved Son, in whom I am well pleased."

In Matthew, befitting the record of Christ's Kingship, His word is one of introduction and authentication: "This is My Son." In Mark and in Luke, the Father says: "Thou art My Son," addressing Him directly, a sweet comfort to the heart of the lowly Servant and the lonely Man.

A second time the Father speaks such words to Him, and this when the last humiliation of the Cross and the stillness of the tomb are left behind forever. With words of triumphant greeting, "Thou art My Son, this day have I begotten Thee" (Heb. 1:5), the Father welcomes Him to the glory of His risen life. Deep was the Father's joy in His beloved One when, in obedience to His will, the Son entered His path of abasement on earth. How deep, then, must be His delight in receiving Him from the dead!

In this way the Sonship of Christ is given its second vindication, for He is "declared to be the Son of God with power, according to the Spirit of holiness, by the resurrection from the dead (Rom. 1:4). Never again shall there be any doubt concerning His glory as the Son of God.

Finally, God's pleasure in Him is such that He is bringing sons to glory, all accepted in the Beloved, and all brought within the clasp of the Father's love. These all shall be conformed to the image of His Son, with a sonship patterned on that of their glorious Lord, though not on the same plane. In peopling heaven with myriads like His Beloved, that in them He may behold His beauty, God bears witness that Christ is the Son of His love.

Thus the Sonship of Christ is His own unique glory. It is His as co-equal and co-eternal with the Father. Dwelling in the perfect intimacy of the Godhead, above all, the Son is the supreme object of the Father's love.

CHAPTER TWO

The Theophanies

Hail Him, ye heirs of David's line,
Whom David "Lord" did call,
The God Incarnate, Man Divine,
And crown Him Lord of all. —E. Perronet

On many occasions in Old Testament history it pleased God to reveal Himself to the astonished gaze of men. With mortal eyes they beheld Him, sometimes manifested in overpowering brightness and at other times in angelic or human guise. To patriarchs, judges, priests, kings, and prophets, to men and women humble yet holy, in Israel or beyond its borders, the vision was given. It surpassed every other delight in the spiritual life. No scenes in the path of these worthies of old are more instructive than those in which God appeared to them displaying glory and grace, holiness and love, power and gentleness. Yet by this very contrast, it also showed up the need and unworthiness of the men and women to whom He deigned to reveal Himself.

While it is true that "no man hath seen God at any time," also true are the words concerning the seventy-four on Sinai: "they saw the God of Israel" (Ex. 24:10). To Moses God said: "Thou canst not see My face: for there shall no man see Me, and live" (Ex. 33:20), yet on another occasion, Moses stated: "Thou Lord art seen face to face" (Num. 14:14).

It is evident, then, that such glimpses of God given to men were partial. He said concerning Moses: "The simili-

tude of the Lord shall he behold" (Num. 12:8). The manifestations of His brightness were limited according to the
lessons He was teaching His people. But no mortal was
allowed to gaze on unshrouded Deity.

Not only does the Scripture record these *theophanies,*
these appearings of God, but it gives weighty evidence that
the Being in whom God was revealed was none other than
the beloved Son. This is implied in the title of our Lord in
the Colossian letter: "the image of the invisible God." By
virtue of His place in the Godhead, the display of the
divine majesty is always in Him. The same lesson is taught
elsewhere in terms that leave no shadow of doubt. John the
Apostle quoted from Isaiah's record of his vision of the
Lord: "These things said Esaias, when he saw His glory,
and spake of Him" (Jn. 12:41). Thus John proclaimed that
it was the Son whom Isaiah beheld and to whom the seraphs gave their homage. Other instances of this same iden-
tification will appear as we proceed through the Old
Testament records.

While we see in the theophanies something of the
majesty which belonged to the Son before the incarnation,
we notice that these were only appearances suited to the
occasion; we must not attribute to the Deity bodily parts or
passions. Even when the appearance was in human guise, it
did not mean that manhood had been taken into union with
Deity. That took place at the incarnation, and only then.

Woven richly into the texture of the early history of
Israel is the record of One who is called the Angel of the
Lord. The title "Angel of the Lord" (i.e. Jehovah), occurs
always in the singular, never in the plural. Angels of God
are many; the Angel of Jehovah is alone in His nature and
deeds.

This in itself stirs our interest, but of far greater moment
is the fact that He wields divine authority, bears divine

names, and receives divine worship. This is borne out by the detail of the narrative of Scripture. The first time we read of this Angel is in Genesis 16. He found Hagar by a fountain of water in the wilderness, and said to her: "I will multiply thy seed exceedingly." Thus she "called the name of the Lord (Jehovah) that spake unto her, Thou God seest me." The Angel is called "Jehovah that spake unto her."

In Genesis 22, when Abraham took the knife to slay his son, bringing to a solemn climax his obedience to the command of God, the Angel of the Lord called to him out of heaven and stopped his hand. The Angel said: "Thou hast not withheld thy son, thine only son from Me." Again, "By Myself have I sworn, saith the Lord...that in blessing I will bless thee...because thou hast obeyed My voice." The voice of the Angel was the voice of the Lord.

To Jacob, too, the Angel manifested Himself in three of the outstanding events of the patriarch's life. When, in Genesis 28, the fugitive slept on the stone at Bethel, he saw in his dream One who said: "I am the Lord God of Abraham...and, behold I am with thee...and will bring thee again into this land." In Genesis 31, One whom Jacob called "the Angel of God" appeared to Him and said: "I am the God of Bethel, where thou anointest the pillar." So the Lord who stood above the ladder was identified with the Angel.

Even more remarkable was the experience at Peniel. "There wrestled a man with him until the breaking of the day." Of this Hosea said: "He had power over the Angel." The Angel changed his name from Jacob to Israel and blessed him there. Jacob realized the greatness of the One who had wrestled with him, sought to know His name, and called the name of the place Peniel, i.e., the face of God, for he said, "I have seen God face to face, and my life is preserved" (Gen. 32).

When Jacob, in the sunset of life, blessed the two sons of Joseph, his word was, "God, before whom my fathers Abraham and Isaac did walk, the God which fed me all my life long unto this day, the Angel which redeemed me from all evil, bless the lads" (Gen. 48:15-16). Surely no created being could be spoken of in such terms.

Few scenes in Israel's history were fraught with wonder equal to that in Exodus 3, where Moses beheld the burning bush. "The Angel of the Lord appeared unto him in a flame of fire out of the midst of the bush," yet "when the Lord saw that he turned aside to see, God called unto him out of the midst of the bush…and He said, Draw not nigh hither: put off thy shoes from off thy feet for the place whereon thou standest is holy ground." From the bush God declared Himself to Moses as the I AM. Thus the Angel is spoken of as Lord and God, whose presence made holy the very ground where His servant stood. Does this not deepen the wonder with which we hear the same One long centuries after speak the same title: "I AM," and that through the pure lips of His stainless manhood?

When the people of Israel left Egypt, "the Lord went before them by day in a pillar of a cloud" (Ex. 13:21), and "the Angel of God, which went before the camp of Israel, removed and went behind them; and the pillar of cloud went from before their face, and stood behind them" (Ex. 14:19). The Angel of the Lord spoke of this at Bochim where He reproved the negligence of the people and said, "I made you to go up out of Egypt" (Jud. 2:1).

In fact, it is in the book of the Judges that we read most fully of the identity of the Angel with the Son of God. To Gideon the Angel of the Lord appeared, and said: "The Lord is with thee," yet in the same conversation, "the Lord looked upon him and said, Go in this thy might." When Gideon sought to do Him honour by his offering, the Angel touched it with his staff and there rose up fire out of the rock and consumed it (Jud. 6:21).

Most remarkable of all was the appearing to Manoah and his wife in Judges 13. The latter spoke of Him as "a man of God" whose countenance was like that of an angel of God, very terrible. When Manoah wished to make an offering to Him, the Angel said, "If thou wilt offer a burnt offering, thou must offer it unto the Lord," for Manoah did not know that He was an Angel of the Lord. The clear implication of these words is that it was proper for the Angel to receive an offering when He was recognized as such. What created being dare receive such an honour? When John in Patmos twice went to worship his angel-guide, the latter on both occasions refused the honour and bade him worship God, but the Angel of Jehovah declined no honour as inappropriate for Him.

When asked by Manoah as to His name, He replied: "Why askest thou thus after My name, seeing it is secret?" But the word "secret" (or wonderful) is one of the names ascribed to our Lord Jesus in Isaiah 9:6. "His Name shall be called Wonderful." Not only was the Angel's name "Wonderful," but He did wondrously in that when the flame went up toward heaven from the altar, He ascended in the flame. Who but One dare add Himself to a sacrifice to the Lord?

In all His dealings, the Angel of the Lord displayed deep concern for the welfare of the people of Israel. He led them in their journeys, encamping round about them that feared Him (see Ps. 34:7). He laid the army of the Assyrians low in death (Isa. 37:36), so that it was true of the people of God: the "Angel of His presence saved them" (Isa. 63:9). He appeared with drawn sword to withstand Balaam so that the perverse prophet fell on his face before Him (Num. 22:31). He revealed Himself to Joshua as Captain of the host of the Lord, accepted worship from him, and bade him stand with unshod feet on such holy ground (Josh. 5:13).

He stood between earth and heaven with drawn sword over Jerusalem when David sinned in numbering the people, and the sword was sheathed only when the sacrifice was offered (1 Chron. 21:16-27). He will be seen again, for Malachi said: "The Lord, whom ye seek, shall suddenly come to His temple, even the Messenger (i.e., Angel) of the covenant, whom ye delight in: behold, He shall come, saith the Lord of hosts. But who may abide the day of His coming?" (Mal. 3:1-2). The true hope of Israel is the return in majesty of the Lord, the Angel of the Covenant. Faithful He ever was; faithful He will ever be.

Can there be any lingering doubt as to His person? Do not these records of His past dealings illumine the words spoken in the temple in Matthew 23:37, "How often would I have gathered thy children together, even as a hen gathereth her chickens under her wings, and ye would not"? He had often preserved them in their history, and often been refused. Now at last He was despised and rejected by men.

There were times when the theophanies were accompanied by profound radiance. Such was the case when Moses, Aaron, Nadab and Abihu, and seventy of the elders of Israel saw the God of Israel (Ex. 24:10); also when Ezekiel by the river Chebar beheld the Lord with His cherubic attendants. In both scenes He was enthroned in sapphire splendour deep in the blaze of heavenly light. By the river Hiddekel, Daniel saw One whose "body also was like the beryl, and His face as the appearance of lightning, and His eyes as lamps of fire, and His arms and His feet like in colour to polished brass, and the voice of His words like the voice of a multitude" (Dan. 10:6). The effect on the prophet was the same as produced by such a vision when seen by the worthiest of men. He was made deeply conscious of his corruption and was prostrated in abasement before the feet of the glorious One.

In none of these scenes was the glory more evident than in Isaiah's glimpse of the majesty of his Lord. When the long reign of Uzziah had ended in the corruption of the tomb, the prophet beheld One whose throne was forever. Seven centuries were to elapse before the occupant of that throne stooped to thirty-three years of deepening humiliation that culminated in the sorrows of the Tree.

But on the day of the vision, He was dwelling in His rightful sphere, sitting on a throne high and lifted up (or lofty) as befitting "the high and lofty One that inhabiteth eternity, whose name is Holy." The flowing robe of His vestment of majesty filled all the temple; there was room in that place for one King, and only one. His sovereignty was absolute; He could not give His glory to another. It must be so. In the temple of the believer's body, as in that of the believing company, there is room for one Lord, and only one.

As a living canopy over the throne stood the seraphs, the burners, aflame with the holiness of the Presence in which they served. With faces hidden in profound reverence as was right before their Lord, and with feet out of sight, as suited the lowly estate of the creature, they waited to fulfil every command. From their lips pealed their adoration, seraph answering to seraph, and with one mind proclaiming the dignity of their Lord. Their "Holy, Holy, Holy" pointed to the mystery of Trinity in Unity, yet all the glory was displayed in One whom Isaiah saw, and whom John identified as the beloved Son. To Him, therefore, belonged the name "Lord of hosts," the name that set forth His high and unapproachable supremacy amid the hierarchies of heaven. His name was Jehovah, proclaiming Him the eternal and unchangeable One.

It is of incalculable profit to our souls to behold the glory of Christ in the theophanies. Throughout both Testaments we see one blessed Person, Himself the perfect revelation of God. All that He was in His dealings with His people in ancient days, He was still in the days of His flesh. The same love that had yearned over them during the long ages of their history, lavished its treasures upon them in His humiliation and death. Nothing could change His heart, as nothing ever shall. Whether as the Angel of the Lord, or as the radiant Sovereign of the heavenly throne, or as the lonely Man of Sorrows, or as the ascended Christ at God's right hand, or as the Lamb in the bliss of the holy Jerusalem, this is the One whom the Spirit of God delights to reveal to our wondering eyes.

CHAPTER THREE

His Eternity

Crown Him the Lord of years,
The Potentate of time,
Creator of the rolling spheres,
Ineffably sublime! —M. Bridges

The sacred page portrays the majesty of our Lord not only as existent before His incarnation but in His eternity, before and above all creation. This is particularly so in the Colossian letter. Colosse was a small decadent town in Asia Minor, where the little assembly no doubt lived in an atmosphere depressing in many respects, and without the possibilities which great cities would afford with the cheering fellowship of many brethren. If in Colosse there was little for the believers, there was everything in Christ. Thus Paul wrote to them the epistle of the fulness of Christ. In the first chapter, we learn His majesty Godward as the Son of His love and as the image of the invisible God. We also learn of His greatness in relation to the universe as the Firstborn of every creature, and regarding His saints as the Head of His body the Church.

The title of Firstborn ascribes to our Lord the pre-eminence of an absolute heirship. In an ancient family, the firstborn possessed the birthright. To him pertained not only a double portion of his father's property but the place of honour among his brethren. All the usage of the term in the Old Testament points to its meaning—priority not only of time but also of rank. So we read: "Thus saith the Lord, Israel is My son, even My firstborn" (Ex. 4:22). Again we read: "I will make him My firstborn, higher than the kings of the earth" (Ps. 89:27).

As applied to our Lord, the title transcends all thought of time, indicating His position as unique in sonship and in inheritance. Because He was always God's Son, loved with everlasting love, He was God's heir—heir before He was Creator. Creation was brought into being to be His inheritance. Therefore this term of dignity looks back to sonship and forward to ownership, and expresses the sovereignty of the Son over all creation. All things exist for Him, and belong to Him.

Far from being part of creation, He was personally distinct from it, as is clear from the following words in the Colossian letter: "For by Him were all things created." The creature has life derived from its Creator; God's firstborn has life in Himself, eternally. As to the creation, we read: "For in Him (R.V.) were all things created, that are in heaven, and that are on earth, visible and invisible, whether they be thrones, or dominions, or principalities, or powers: all things were created by Him, and for Him."

These three phrases are worthy of special note: in Him; by Him; and for Him.

In Him were the power and the reason for creation. In Him was the power which from Himself alone could summon a universe into being, fashioning space and time as the very conditions of its existence. In Him was the reason for its being: that due to His sonship the Father's love should bestow on Him such a portion.

In Him, too, was the meaning of each thing created. It would show Him forth, as for example, the dignity of the noonday sun and of the mountain peak, and the value of the fruitful tree, or it would provide the fitting scene for the working out of His purposes, even as the waves of the sea were fashioned for the treading of His feet.

By Him: His was the agency which created all things from the mighty seraph to the lowly stone. His work displayed perfection of order, and proceeded on an ascending scale of beauty and design. A wise and loving purpose placed each form of life in harmony with its environment. His vastness of design gave to His handiwork such dimension that astronomers speak in terms of light-years, and seek to guess at the motion through space of faroff nebulae by the colour of their spectrum.

His was the skill which gave to the atom the structure that entrances the physicist, and bound into its being the energy which has so startled our modern world. His intelligence fashioned man's mind with all its intricacy, and gave to the acorn power to produce the oak tree.

As we ponder the wonders of the universe, losing ourselves either in the immensity of the starry spaces or in the exquisite workmanship of the tiniest things, it is a relief to look up to their source, the Maker. "Lo, these are parts of His ways: but how little a portion is heard of Him" (Job 26:14). Yet through grace we know Him personally as our own beloved Saviour, and are called to the sweetness and privilege of an intimate relationship with Him.

For Him: Christ is the end as well as the beginning, the goal as well as the source. All things exist for His sake, not arbitrarily, but by virtue of His infinite goodness and wisdom. Not even the rebellion of sin can hinder this. The lost shall be monuments eternally of His longsuffering and of His power, even as the saved are—of His grace and mercy.

Not only so, but "He is (not was) before all things, and in Him all things consist" (R.V.). In Him all things are bound together by one power and one purpose, thus making the universe an ordered whole. Not only has He started creation on its journey, but He maintains it age after age. It is never out of control. Never for one moment have the forces of evil been able to pass the limits set by the permissive will of the One who says: "Hitherto shalt thou come, but no further." At last the goal shall be reached when every created intelligence shall acknowledge Jesus as Lord to the glory of God the Father, and the righteousness of His ways, both in mercy and in judgment, shall be vindicated before every eye.

A similarly precious truth is brought before us in the vision given to John on Patmos. There the Lord revealed Himself to His servant as the First and the Last. Behind John's exile and all his tribulation, behind the seemingly tangled course of the years, behind all the mystery of the sovereignty of God, stood the glorious figure of the Eternal One. Well might He lay His hand on His servant and speak the words that banished fear.

His words of power and peace have their special comfort for our own day. In each of the seven letters to the churches of Asia in Revelation 2 and 3, the Lord Jesus describes Himself in terms peculiarly suited to the need of the church addressed. These letters not only deal with the immediate need of local churches in the apostles' day, but also span the history of the whole Church until the Lord's return. So we note with deep interest that in the letter to Laodicea, the last of the seven, the Lord affirms Himself to be the beginning of the creation of God.

How much we need this reminder who live so near to the close of the Church's pilgrimage, in a day when the theory of evolution has obscured men's minds, and produced much havoc in marred lives and lost souls. He who knew our circumstances from eternity has warned us in our day by this very Scripture to hold fast to the certainty of His creative majesty. As the Beginning, He is the Fount of creation, its active cause, not part of it. Thus amid deepening apostasy, we are called to depend on the One who brought all things into existence and who will yet bring the universe to its appointed destiny.

The eternal majesty of our Lord shines out brightly in Hebrews 1. He is the Son who is appointed heir of all things and by whom the ages are made. Having achieved redemption, He takes His seat at the right hand of the Majesty on high. He is inducted into His inheritance as God's firstborn (v. 6) and saluted as God. The heavens are the works of His hands, and though they perish, He remains—the same yesterday, and today, and forever.

However it is not only that our beloved Saviour is the maker of the starry hosts, not only that He upholds (i.e., bears on surely to the goal) all things by the word of His power. It is also true that when the heavens "shall wax old as doth a garment," and He shall "fold them up as a vesture, and they shall be changed," He Himself will abide, unchanged and unchangeable. What is the majesty of such a Being who puts on a universe for the accomplishment of His purposes, and puts it off again, changing it as we might a garment?

Throughout the changing manifestations of His glory, even in the years of His humiliation and suffering, He remains the same blessed Person. Throughout the changes of His people's history with their experiences of joy and of sorrow, of failure and of triumph, He remains the same. Through the long drama of things in earth and things in heaven, their defilement by sin and their reconciliation through the Cross, the Lord Jesus Himself knows no change. Even through that mighty change when the first heaven and the first earth pass away to reveal the new heaven and the new earth, He is the same. Though change and decay is the order of things around us, we look beyond them to the abiding One who fills both time and eternity.

Great as is this vista of His majesty, a greater is seen in

the prophecy of Isaiah 9:6, "For unto us a Child is born, unto us a Son is given: and the government shall be upon His shoulder, and His Name shall be called Wonderful, Counsellor, the mighty God, the everlasting Father, the Prince of Peace." We note the title "everlasting Father," or "Father of Eternity" (R.V., marg.). The word "father" is used in the Old Testament for the author of anything, of its nourisher and preserver, and also of the one who excels in any particular quality. As applied here to our Lord, it expresses His creative majesty as the author of the ages, and His upholding power as the sustainer of their history. It indicates His fixity of purpose in respect to the whole procession of creation, and the progress and destiny of the creature. With wise and fatherly care, He has respect to the work of His hands, and seeks only good for it.

As the context of the passage brings before us His perfect reign, so the title opens to us a vista of the future, of an eternal order which will supersede this world's sorry systems. It will be founded on righteousness wrought by the atoning Cross, will be characterized by peace, and will know neither curse nor corruption. Of that eternity of bliss for all His redeemed, our Lord is the author. Moreover, the title shows Him as the One who is peculiarly marked by the possession of eternity in Himself. In Isaiah 57:15, He is "the high and lofty One that inhabiteth eternity, whose name is Holy." There, He dwells in eternity. In Isaiah 9:6, eternity dwells in Him! To Him we might well address the words of adoration:

> *No age can heap its outward years on Thee.*
> *Blest Lord! Thou art Thyself Thine own eternity.*

It is not merely pre-existence which belongs to Christ, but eternity. We listen with awe to the words spoken to the unbelieving Jews as He taught in the temple: "Before

Abraham was, I am" (Jn. 8:58). He identified Himself with the One who had spoken to Moses from the bush, and had proclaimed Himself: "I AM THAT I AM" (Ex. 3). On the part of the Jews, there was no doubt as to what He claimed. Rejecting its truth, they could only accuse Him of blasphemy, taking up stones to stone Him.

Far more than existence before Abraham was claimed. This would have been indicated had He said: "Before Abraham was, I was," but His word was: "I AM." This existence was independent of all thought of time. With Him essentially there is no past and no future, but rather an eternal present. Time, like space, is a condition belonging to the creature. Our Lord Jesus, who in His perfect wisdom bound such limitations into our finite being, is Himself beyond and above them.

Thus He revealed Himself in unapproachable majesty and in the glory of a self-sufficient life. He appropriated this title in the days of His flesh, amid humiliation, scorn, and contempt. Let us never forget that when He stood under the cruel scourge, surrounded by extreme indignity, and when He hung in direst shame and anguish on the awful tree, it was with full consciousness of His eternal majesty and of His timeless Being.

What was the joy of His eternal past, of that glory which He had with the Father before the world was? In Isaiah 6 (with Jn. 12:41) we find that the seraphs adored Him with veiled faces, saying, "Holy, Holy, Holy is the Lord of Hosts," but this was homage paid by His creatures. His was majesty before creation. His was equality with God, equality both of nature and of state. His was the perfect fellowship of the Word with God (Jn. 1:1), the intimacy of a life rich beyond all creature understanding. His was, as it ever is, the bliss of sonship, the joy of that abode of love, the bosom of the Father. His was the eternal joy of knowing that the Father's love had given Him those who would be with Him to behold His glory, the glory that would follow the bearing of the curse. We close this meditation on the eternal glory of Christ with words that should bow us before Him in loving adoration: "Ye know the grace of our Lord Jesus Christ, that, though He was rich, yet for your sakes He became poor that ye through His poverty might be rich" (2 Cor. 8:9).

CHAPTER FOUR

His Deity

*"A Saviour not quite God is a bridge broken at the
farther end."* —H. C. G. Moule

Far from being a matter of academic discussion, the
truth of our Lord's Deity is vital to our salvation. When we
bow before our God, and think of what He is, in the vastness of His eternity and in the intensity of His holiness, our
hearts cry out for One who shall "lay His hand upon us
both," reaching down to our lowliness and up to God's sub-
limity. Nor do we cry out in vain, for we find this One in
our Lord Jesus Christ, the incarnate Word. He is as truly
God as man, and as truly man as God.

A perfect Saviour cannot be less than God. Only Deity
could sustain the burden of those works which our Lord
undertook when He stooped to save. Our Saviour must possess full Deity to be the effective sin-bearer, satisfying forever the claims of the holiness of God; to be the true mediator, comprehending the depths of God as well as the needs
of man; to be the revealer in whom God could be fully
known; to be the exhaustless Fount of bliss to His own.

Our purpose in this chapter is to ponder some of the
titles given to our Lord in the Scripture regarding His relation to God. Though they are only part of the rich portrayal
of Christ's majesty, they contribute their wealth of witness
to the glory of His Person. They combine to present to us
One on whom our souls may lean in that perfect rest which
the creature finds only in the Creator, and the finite in the
infinite and eternal.

The Brightness of His Glory (Heb. 1:3): The term "glory" is used here in its widest sense, as being the radiant fulness of the excellencies of God, including all the splendour of His nature and character. God's glory endures forever (Ps. 104:31), whereas man's glory is as the flower of grass which falls away (1 Pet. 1:24). Human glory is vain and transient; the divine is substantial and eternal. Haman of old could boast of the glory of his riches, but God possesses riches of glory.

> ...*Thine, Lord, is majesty,*
> *By time undimmed, nor as earth's pageantry;*
> *No bound nor measure doth Thy glory know—*
> *Past searching out its vast eternal flow.*

The Father is the living fount of this glory and the Son is the living stream. The Son is the brightness, the effulgence, the outshining of the glory, so that the relationship between the Father and the Son has intimacy like to that between the light and the ray that streams from it. As is the light, so is the ray, and neither exists without the other. As are the holiness, the love, and grace of the Father, so are those of the Son. Indeed all the glories of God shine forth unchanged in Christ, undimmed in their lustre, fadeless in their beauty, and constant in their ardour.

Moreover, light may be known only through its own rays, so God may be known only through Christ. Our Lord in His eternal being, apart altogether from the changing manifestations of His own majesty, is uniquely and exclusively the outshining of the glory of God.

Nothing short of equality of nature is set forth in this identical possession of the riches of glory. Therefore to have Christ is to have everything in Him. Rich indeed is the Scripture which tells us: "Christ Jesus...is made unto us wisdom, and righteousness, and sanctification, and redemption" (1 Cor. 1:30). He Himself has been made to us all these things. His own fulness is their only measure. With deep reverence we therefore say that God could not bless us more than He has done. He has given us Christ, His supreme treasure, "riches none may count or tell." He has given us Christ, and in this unspeakable gift has given us all that He Himself is.

The Express Image of His Person (Heb. 1:3): The word translated "express image" means "to engrave, or cut into," and is used especially of the impression made by a die, as in the stamping of coins. The impression reproduces exactly the features on the face of the die. To see the one is to see the other. Then the term "person" refers to that which "lies under," not to outward appearance, but to inward reality. The Son is the express image of God's Person, the perfect display of all that is essential to the being of God.

Here, then, He is seen as of one substance with the Father, yet personally distinct from Him. In the Son is set forth every quality, every resource, every power that dwells in God. Therefore to behold the Son is to behold the Father.

This precious truth we have from the lips of the Lord Jesus Himself. We recall the words which He spoke in the upper room: "He that hath seen Me hath seen the Father" (Jn. 14:9). Knowing the Son, we know the Father; not vaguely but in truth. Beholding the face wet with tears by the tomb of Lazarus, we see that the Father is compassionate; beholding the unsullied purity of that life, we learn that the Father is holy; beholding the sufferings of the Cross, we learn that the Father is loving.

Nor is it otherwise when we see the embrace that folded the little children to His heart, and the intense longing with which He gazed on the weary multitudes. We listen to the voice whose words of comfort healed many a broken heart, and opened paradise to a dying thief. In these, as in the

many other scenes which throng the memory with rich
blessing, we learn to know God, and our hearts are satisfied
indeed.

"He that hath seen Me hath seen the Father." These
words were His gracious response to the request of Philip:
"Lord, show us the Father, and it sufficeth us." Though the
apostle's statement showed how little he had read the meaning of the Lord's path, yet it was of deep moment for it is
the first time in the New Testament when the word "Father"
rested on a disciple's lips. Philip spoke truly of the only
object which could be a sufficient vision. Men's eyes are
hungry. They look for more and more to meet their desire.
Never does the eye say: "It is enough," for such cannot be
until God is seen to be revealed in Christ. We bow our
hearts and say: "We have seen the Father—our Father; it
certainly is enough."

The Image of the Invisible God (Col. 1:15): In the Son
alone God is fully seen. This is an eternal necessity, arising
not from the frailty of the creature, but from the very
nature of God. Such is the relationship between the Persons
of the Trinity that in the Son is all the manifestation of
God. This is brought out in the title before us. The term
"image" speaks of a resemblance that is derived, and of a
likeness not of mere similarity but of identity of nature.
Such is the likeness that God, with infinite delight, beholds
in His Son, the perfect mirror of His own character. Every
depth in Him is met by answering depth in the Son. The
love with which He regards His Beloved is reciprocated by
like love on the part of the Son. All His thoughts of grace
to unworthy sinners find their perfect response in like
thoughts in the heart of Him who is His image.

Not only does God behold in Christ His own likeness,
but we gaze on that living mirror and in it see the entirety
of the divine revelation. In Christ God is fully displayed,

with a display that is always in the Son. The expression "who is the image" is akin to that two verses later: "He is before all things" in that the present tense is used of that which is beyond all time.

We have noted that it was the Son who was seen in the appearances of God in the Old Testament, not then incarnate, but indeed pre-existent. In the days of His flesh He was still the image of the invisible God, as He is now in His glorified state. In the ages to come, He will still be the visible manifestation of God, for in his description of the Holy City, John says: "The throne of God and of the Lamb shall be in it; and His servants shall serve Him: and they shall see His face" (Rev. 22:3-4). Thus in the face that once was wreathed with deepest agony, we shall see the glory of the Godhead—of Father, Son, and Holy Spirit. It is in every sense most fitting that the display of the divine majesty should be on the visage that was more marred than any man.

The Word (Jn. 1:1): This term even more vividly shows that our Lord Jesus is the complete revelation of God. The Word is that by which God expresses what He is. It is not that our Lord bears the revelation of God, but that, far more, He is Himself that very revelation. It is not that He is the messenger alone, but that He is the very message. As such, He is the full and ultimate answer to every longing of the soul that seeks to know God.

If, like David in the wilderness, we exclaim: "My soul thirsteth for Thee, my flesh longeth after Thee," and like Moses at Sinai: "That I may know Thee," and like Paul in Rome: "That I may know Him," we shall not be disappointed. Paul could glory that the Son of God whom he preached "was not yea and nay, but in Him was yea" (2 Cor. 1:19). Never had the apostle to hang his head and confess reluctantly that there was not enough in his Saviour to meet the need of any stricken soul. "In Him was yea." He was the positive God-given answer to every human need.

The perfection of Christ as the revelation finds its secret in His relation to God. John opens his Gospel with a glimpse of the dignity of the everlasting Word. Moses in Genesis started with: "In the beginning God created," and later spoke of the Lord God who breathed into man's nostrils the breath of life. John starts: "In the beginning was the Word...all things were made by Him," and later portrays Christ in resurrection as the breather of life, indeed the Lord God of the new creation. Moses went back to the initial point of creation, but John goes far beyond it, for when all things created came into existence from their mighty source, the Word already was. Again, "the Word was with God," not as co-existent only, but in the wealth of measureless communion. Finally, "the Word was God," possessing the very nature of Deity.

Christ is the living Word. Tauler, in the Middle Ages, put it enigmatically when he said: "God hath spoken but one Word, and that Word is still unspoken." All God's message is forever comprehended in Christ, so that all we can ever know, or need to know, is in Him. As all this is given in a living person, the message is always a present one. Such must it eternally be; there can be no end to the telling forth of God in Christ.

To the use of these titles we may add the divine name given to the Son. In the Old Testament, God was set forth as the eternal and unchangeable One who deigned to link Himself in covenant with His people. This was told out in His name JEHOVAH. This name was held in such profound reverence by the Jews that they refrained from pronouncing it. Where the text of the Old Testament had Jehovah, they read Adonai. If, then, the writers of the New Testament apply to the Lord Jesus' quotations from the Old

Testament using the name Jehovah, it is with complete conviction as to His Deity. The Old Testament prepared the way for this in such a passage as: "Jehovah rained upon Sodom and Gomorrah brimstone and fire from Jehovah out of heaven" (Gen. 19:24). There two Persons arc indicated, each bearing the sacred name.

John the apostle quotes from Isaiah concerning the latter's vision of his Lord, and says: "These things said Esaias, when he saw His glory, and spoke of Him" (Jn. 12:41). Thus John proclaims Christ to be the One of whom the seraphs said: "Holy, Holy, Holy is Jehovah of hosts."

Again, in Isaiah 8:13-14, we read: "Sanctify Jehovah of Hosts Himself...and He shall be...for a stone of stumbling and for a rock of offence." Peter shows that Christ is that stone and that rock, and therefore Jehovah (see 1 Pet. 2:7-8). In the temptation, Christ quoted the words of the law: "Thou shalt worship the Lord thy God, and Him only shalt thou serve," where the text of the Old Testament had "Jehovah thy God." Nevertheless He received worship at various times, and never declined it. Thus He proclaimed Himself to be Jehovah of hosts.

Further, we note eight occasions when the Scripture expressly calls Christ God:

1. "His name shall be called Wonderful, Counsellor, the mighty God, the everlasting Father, the Prince of Peace" (Isa. 9:6). In this unmistakable prophecy of the One who shall rule on the throne of David, He is given a five-fold name. Its first two parts kindle our awe and lead us up to the central one; the last two flow from it as its sublime sequences. The weight of emphasis rests thus on the expression: "The mighty God."

2. "They shall call His name Emmanuel, which being interpreted is, God with us" (Mt. 1:23). Here is a quotation from the prophecy in Isaiah 6 of the birth of the virgin's

Son. The weak and unbelieving King Ahaz was bidden to ask of the Lord his God a sign either in the depth or in the height above. Ahaz refused to ask, whereupon God gave the sign, one indeed which should be both in the depth and in the height above. Well is it that our Lord is Emmanuel— God with us. We see Him in the depth when He is made sin for us; we see Him in the height when He is exalted far above all heavens. Both on the Cross and on the Throne the immensity of His work is such that only Deity is sufficient for its accomplishment.

3. "The Word was God" (Jn. 1:1). This designation has already been discussed earlier in the chapter.

4. "My Lord and my God" (Jn. 20:28). When Thomas beheld the risen Lord, he was as emphatic in his homage as previously in his unbelief. He heard the gracious words that drew his gaze to the pierced hands and the riven side. Then looking into the face that once had been crowned with thorns and into the eyes that once had glistened with human tears, he saw his God. The words of adoration burst forth spontaneously. In his devotion there could be no reserves. For him the Crucified was henceforth both Lord and God.

5. "Christ came, who is over all, God blessed forever" (Rom. 9:5). Paul enumerates the privileges given to Israel as a nation, and brings the list to its climax in the crowning favour shown to that people, that through them Christ came in the flesh. What made His birth through Israel to be the supreme glory of the nation was the fact that He was far more than of Davidic line; He is God blessed forever. In the very words of this brief but expressive doxology, Paul pays to Him the same honour which he pays to the Father in his praise in the Ephesian Epistle: "Blessed be the God and Father of our Lord Jesus Christ."

6. "Looking for the blessed hope and appearing of the

glory of our great God and Saviour Jesus Christ, who gave Himself for us (Titus 2:13-14, R.V.). The rendering of the Revised Version is consistent with the obvious truth that He whom we shall see appearing in glory is our Lord Jesus Christ. The glory will be the fitting manifestation of the eternal dignity of His own Person. The word "great" reminds us that Peter speaks of having been "an eye-witness of His majesty," i.e., His excellent greatness (2 Pet. 1:16). He who gave Himself for us, stooping to the dread humiliation of His atoning death, is none other than our great God.

7. "Thy Throne, O God, is for ever and ever" (Heb. 1:8). It is the Father who speaks thus to the Son. He has said: "Thou art My Son, this day have I begotten Thee," and now He addresses Him: "Thy Throne, O God..." Here, then, is no mere ascription by any creature of divine honour to Christ.

8. "This is the true God, and eternal life" (1 Jn. 5:20). At the commencement of his epistle, John says: "We show unto you that eternal life, which was with the Father, and was manifested unto us." Now his task reaches its close, and he says of the One whose manifestation he has so described: "This is the true God, and eternal life." We are in "Him that is true"; that is, we are in the Father because we are in His Son Jesus Christ. The teaching of John is one, whether in his Gospel, or in this epistle—Christ is God.

Thus in the titles which together set forth the unique dignity of Christ as the revelation of God, in His own rightful possession of the name Jehovah, and in the reiterated application to Him of the name of God, we see how ample is Scripture's witness to the fulness of His Deity. This Deity is always His, alike on the Throne and on the Cross. It is His now upon whom we believe, and shall be His for evermore.

"In Him dwelleth all the fulness of the Godhead bodily" (Col. 2:9). We rejoice in such a Saviour, and adore Him as our Lord and our God.

CHAPTER FIVE

His Incarnation

Come now and view that manger—
The Lord of Glory see,
A houseless, homeless Stranger,
In this poor world, for thee.

There see the Godhead glory
Shine through that human veil;
And willing, hear the story
Of love that's come to heal. —J. N. Darby

The central mystery of our faith is the Person of our Lord Jesus Christ. Before this burning bush we stand with unshod feet, beholding true and holy manhood linked with eternal Deity. How the two are united in the one Person lies beyond the comprehension of the creature, for "no man knoweth the Son but the Father" (Mt. 11:27). Ours is to believe, not to explain, and to worship, not to explore. To attempt any explanation of this wondrous union is to court spiritual disaster. To acknowledge its verities and to bow before the majesty of the Person is to rejoice with joy unspeakable and full of glory. The Incarnation itself is aglow with the grace of a stoop beyond anything that mortals might ever experience. We are invited to ponder reverently its historic facts, the consequent fulness of Christ's Person, and the nearness into which He entered to us.

The Historic Facts: Throughout the Old Testament, promise was added to promise concerning the Coming One, the Seed of the woman who would bruise the serpent's head. Lowliness and greatness, suffering and joy, humiliation and exaltation are woven together in these prophecies. He in whom all these should be fulfilled must therefore combine in His own experience unapproachable heights of fellowship with God and awful depths of solitary anguish.

Of all these promises the first to be quoted in the New Testament concerns His birth: "Behold, a virgin shall be with child, and shall bring forth a son, and they shall call His name Emmanuel, which being interpreted is, God with us" (Mt. 1:23; Isa. 7:14). As the fulfillment of this drew near, a lowly, believing maiden of Davidic ancestry was told by the angel Gabriel that she would bring forth a son and call His name Jesus. This son would be called the Son of the Highest, the Son of God. What would bring the birth to pass? The angel said: "The Holy Ghost shall come upon thee, and the power of the Highest shall overshadow thee" (Lk. 1:26-35). Matthew records that Mary was found with child of the Holy Ghost. Thus, by the power of the Spirit of God, the virgin brought forth One who was "of the seed of David according to the flesh," yet was so truly the Son of God that His name was called Emmanuel. Except for the one fact that Mary bowed to the message from heaven in humble acquiescence, the birth of the Redeemer was wrought entirely by the will and power of God.

There was also the promise concerning the place of His birth: "But thou, Bethlehem-Ephratah, though thou be little among the thousands of Judah, yet out of thee shall He come forth unto Me that is to be ruler in Israel; whose goings forth have been from of old, from everlasting" (Mic. 5:2). This was fulfilled when, in the over-ruling of God, the decree of the Roman Emperor concerning taxation brought Mary and Joseph to Bethlehem. There Mary brought forth her son, "and laid Him in a manger, because there was no room for them in the inn." Earth can always make suitable room for its own great ones, but it had only a manger for Him who was at once too high and too humble to be ranked among such. And later, when wise men came from the east to worship the One who was born King of the Jews (indeed the only One who was ever born a king), both Herod and all Jerusalem with him were troubled by the tidings. Yet no priest nor scribe seems to have visited Bethlehem, and Herod's only interest was a blend of jealousy and murder. In the heart of the rulers, as in the inn, there was no room for Israel's Messiah. Has earth more room for Him today?

To the shepherds in the neighbouring fields the angel of the Lord spoke, saying: "Unto you is born this day in the city of David a Saviour, which is Christ the Lord" (Lk. 2:11). So wondrous to the hosts above was the stoop of their Creator Sovereign to the lowly estate of manhood, that in multitude they appeared and voiced their praise. They spoke of glory to God in the highest, adding fresh lustre to His Throne because of the loving purpose of Him who for a season had left its splendour.

Emmanuel! Emmanuel! I know thy lowly birth;
Thine advent was not heralded by trump or song of earth,
But a watcher and an holy one from heavenly glory came,
With a legion of the shining host, that advent to proclaim.

Rightly did the angel speak of His Person. He was born the Lord, being as truly such in the manger as in the past eternity. Thus did He come forth:

(a) *From Bethlehem,* as to His manifestation in flesh.

(b) *From of old,* as to His dealings with Israel, for He it was who brought the nation out of Egypt.

(c) *From everlasting* ("the days of eternity," Mic. 5:2, Marg.) as to His place with God, in the beginning, before all creation.

In his sublime unfolding of the mind of Christ in Philippians 2, Paul opens to us the facts of the Incarnation by describing three steps in our Lord's path.

1. Though unchangeably in the form of God, He did not look on His equality with God as a prize to be held fast. This refers not to His equality of nature with God, but to that of circumstances and of state from which He parted Himself for the years of His earthly sojourn. This was the glory which He had with the Father before the world was, and for which He prayed before He ascended back to heaven. The form of God He did not lay aside. This form, the very way in which Deity necessarily exists, and therefore involving the nature of Deity, was essentially His after His birth as much as before it. Adoringly we recognize that our Lord Jesus Christ passed through the momentous events of His Incarnation and of His Passion in the unassailable possession of the fulness of the Godhead.

2. Leaving this equality of circumstance, He made Himself of no reputation. This He did by taking on Him the form of a bondservant, which form He took by being made in the likeness of men. He did not become the bondservant in relation to men, but only to God. To them He ministered in lowly grace, but to the will of God He rendered obedience that knew no faltering from the manger to the Cross. It was a path of deep abasement. Except where His greatness was revealed by the Father to believing hearts, it was altogether unrecognized. "He was in the world, and the world was made by Him, and the world knew Him not. He came unto His own, and His own received Him not" (Jn. 1:10-11). Had the Jews believed the Scripture, they would have believed Him and accorded Him a royal welcome. As it was, He walked unknown by the many, for the form of the servant veiled the form of God, and the lowly manhood hid the intrinsic excellence of Deity.

3. Being found in fashion as a man, He shared sinless human experience. In His manhood He toiled as men toiled, partook of their food, and dressed as they dressed. He humbled Himself, in the personal act of a perfect will, by becoming obedient unto death, even to death on the Cross. Thus He who at the beginning of His earthly path stooped from the throne to the manger, at its end stooped from the experience proper to that holy manhood down to the fathomless depths of Calvary's woe.

The Consequent Fulness of His Person: "The Word was made flesh, and dwelt among us (and we beheld His glory, the glory as of the Only begotten of the Father), full of grace and truth" (Jn. 1:14). The Word who was in the beginning, who was with God and was God, became incarnate, yet He who dwelt among men was still the Word. In Person, He remained all that He had ever been, and yet became that which He had never been. He became flesh by taking to Himself all that pertained to true manhood—human spirit, human soul, and human body—yet all apart from sin.

Though His outward circumstances were so greatly altered, yet He remained the Word. His personality was unchanged. To fulness of Deity was added fulness of humanity, and henceforth He possessed two natures, the divine and the human, yet remained one Person. The human nature did not act independently of the divine, nor the divine of the human. All His acts were the acts of His one indivisible Person, acting in the rich possession of the fulness of both natures.

He walked among men in meekness and lowliness, yet was Jehovah's fellow, as in the prophecy which the Lord of Hosts spoke of Him as "the Man that is My fellow" (Zech. 13:7). The communion which He enjoyed with the Father was essentially one, whether in the majesty of heaven's high throne, or in the lowly dependence of His prayers on earth. Thus He could lift His eyes to heaven, yet speak in the full consciousness of His glory which He had with the Father before the world was. Thus could He make request, yet take upon His lips words which the holiest of His people could not dare to utter: "Father, I will" (Jn. 17:1, 5, 24).

The Word dwelt [tabernacled] among men, and that tabernacle was glory-filled. The apostles gazed intently upon that glory which was personally His as the Only begotten of the Father. It shone out in every act and word, in the grace that quenched the thirst of the needy woman by Sychar's well as truly as in the making of water into wine. It was seen in the tears by the grave of Lazarus as truly as in the word of power that raised the dead.

As to the first of those works which we call Christ's miracles, John said: "This beginning of His signs did Jesus in Cana of Galilee, and manifested His glory" (Jn. 2:11, R.V.). John saw in Him far more than a worker of miracles; he recognized the Only Begotten. By enablement of God, such men as Moses and Joshua, Elijah and Elisha, and later the apostles themselves, wrought miracles; but Christ wrought them as signs of His own Person, and in them displayed His own glory.

To opened eyes His glory was most real, even though He was found in fashion as a man. At the marriage feast and at the feeding of the five thousand, He was proclaimed as the divine Creator, able to produce food and drink for His creatures either by the normal processes of nature that depended on His sustaining power, or by the intervention of His sovereign will that dispensed with them at His pleasure. On the troubled sea and beside the tomb, He showed the majesty of an absolute mastery over every opposing thing. Neither the turbulence of the waves nor the corruption of death could thwart His word or hinder His purposes.

Furthermore, His voice was supreme in the unseen world, and brought back the soul to its dwelling in the body.

The glory was seen in His knowledge even as in His power. He knew alike the godly exercise of Nathaniel's heart and the hidden shame of the Samaritan woman. He gave direct answer to the unspoken thoughts of Simon the Pharisee, and showed the woman who touched the hem of His garment that no throng could hide from Him. Before His gaze was spread the local and the distant, the past and the future, the temporal and the eternal.

The Word became flesh, not for a season, but forever. We shall see Him in the midst of the throne, "a Lamb as it had been slain," bearing the marks of Calvary, yet possessing all the attributes of Deity. The Throne itself will belong to God and to the Lamb. Thus the purposes of the Incarnation lay hold both on time and eternity. Far-reaching they are, including the whole scope of our Lord's mediatorial dignity and ministry. These very purposes demand One in whom Deity and humanity shall be indissolubly united, and are forever met in the fulness of our beloved Saviour.

His Nearness to His People: "Forasmuch then as the children are partakers of flesh and blood, He also Himself likewise took part of the same...For verily He took not on Him the nature of angels; but He took on Him the seed of Abraham. Wherefore in all things it behoved Him to be made like unto His brethren" (Heb. 2:14-17). So near did He come to His people that the revelation of God in Him was entirely suited to their apprehension. Had He come in the blaze of heavenly light, they must have remained afar off, stricken with trembling and bewilderment. They were men, not angels, and required just that which His grace gave them—an appearing in pure and sweet and noble manhood. It was not that His lowliness kept His greatness from them. On the contrary, the riches of His infinite

Person were brought to them, and they enjoyed in varying degrees a close and intimate walk with Him.

This may be illustrated from the record of Elisha. In the prophet's yearning for the restoration of life to the dead boy, "he lay upon the child, and put his mouth upon his mouth, and his eyes upon his eyes, and his hands upon his hands: and he stretched himself upon the child" (2 Ki. 4:34). The utmost to which the grown man could attain in nearness to the frame of the child was that mouth should touch mouth, eyes should touch eyes, and hands should touch hands.

Here we may see dimly the grace in which our Lord stooped in coming near to us. His lips spoke words which were life-giving, and fraught with divine blessing, yet they were human lips. From His eyes the depths of Godhead looked out in tireless love on the weary hearts around Him, yet those were human eyes. His hands rested in healing power on the leper, and drew Peter from the clutches of the waves, yet they were human hands.

His lips answered to the lips of His frail people, His eyes to their eyes, and His hands to their hands. All this brought Him near, and enabled a true sharing in the experiences of their life, except in their sinfulness and its ensuing need and corruption.

Such was His nearness to His people that Scripture speaks even of His weakness. "Though He was crucified through weakness, yet He liveth by the power of God" (2 Cor. 13:4). Did His people know hunger, thirst, weariness, and pain? Then He would share these very things; indeed it was in this way that He evidenced the reality of His manhood. This weakness must not be thought of as implying any incapacity, such as ours is when we are unable to withstand the onslaught of death. His was the weakness of a voluntarily accepted capacity for suffering. Our weakness is a condition of our inherent frailty, but His was assumed in the self-humbling of the Incarnation.

Our Lord's holy body was a temple in which the divine glory always dwelt, yet in that temple there hung, as it were, a beautiful veil. Of this we read in Hebrews 10:20, "The veil, that is to say, His flesh," and in Hebrews 5:7, "in the days of His flesh." The latter reference obviously limits the thought to our Lord's path from birth to death. His was "the body of His flesh" (Col. 1:22); now it is "the body of His glory" (Phil. 3:21, R.V.).

This special usage of the word "flesh" sets before us not His body, but His capacity for suffering and death which were associated with His body up to the Cross. This veil the Lord took to Himself in birth that it might be "rent" in Him in death. Even as the veil of old that hid the holiest was beautifully wrought, so the Lord displayed the beauty and perfection of all the ways of God even in the various aspects of His weakness.

Thus did the Lord Jesus become wonderfully near to His people. Sharing with them their daily life and entering into their joys and their sorrows, He brought to them the fulness of His Person. Not only did they know the reality of His humanity, and the signs that attested His Deity, but they knew Him in whom both natures were united. All their association with Him was sacred privilege. They walked and conversed and ate and drank with the One by whom all things were made. Yet He had stooped to all this and even to death itself that He might be known by them and might meet every need of their heart.

At length, one of them who so appreciated His love that he desired to be known only as "the disciple whom Jesus loved," was drawn so near to his Lord that in the upper room on the eve of the Cross, he "lay on Jesus' breast." Such was the privilege given to John that he, a mortal man, was permitted to pillow his head on the bosom of the incarnate God. Such was his experience; such, too, may be ours in spirit who have obtained like precious faith.

CHAPTER SIX

His Humanity

A Man of Sorrows, of toil and tears,
An outcast Man and a lonely—
But He looked on me, and through endless years
Him must I love—Him only.   —Frances Bevan

For thirty-three years the Lord Jesus displayed to the gaze of men a life of incomparable grace and charm. Passing through the various stages of infancy, childhood, youth and manhood, He lived a life so rich in human experience that none who knew Him could ever entertain a doubt as to the reality of His human nature. His years were not spent far from the company of men with only rare appearances which might give rise to vague and misty conceptions of His Person. On the contrary, His earlier life was passed in Nazareth amid the circumstances customary to a godly home. He made such contacts with the people around as were afforded by the trade of the carpenter's shop and by the gatherings in the synagogue.

The period of His public ministry brought Him before the scrutiny of vast crowds, in which jealousy and distrust moved side by side with devotion and love. In such an atmosphere, any unreality or any seeming discrepancy between His claims and His character would have been proclaimed eagerly by His foes. That they should be silent on such matters in spite of the bitter criticism with which they surrounded Him is no small testimony to the glory of His manhood.

The fulness of humanity involves the possession of its

three spheres of being—spirit, soul and body—and all these, with the experience proper to them, are shown to belong to our Lord by the express language of Scripture. All four of the Gospels tell of His human spirit. While Matthew refers only to its being yielded up in death, Mark relates that "Jesus perceived in His spirit" the reasonings in the hearts of the scribes (2:8), and that "He sighed deeply in His spirit" when the Pharisees sought of Him a sign from heaven (8:12).

Luke portrays its gladness, in that "Jesus rejoiced in spirit" when He gave thanks to the Father for the dealings of His will (10:21). John shows us its grief, for when the Lord saw Mary and the Jews weeping before they went to the tomb of the much-loved brother, "He groaned in the spirit, and was troubled" (11:33). When at the paschal meal He beheld the tragedy of Judas, "He was troubled in spirit," and spoke of the betrayal (13:21). Finally, Luke narrates the last words from the Lord's lips as He passed from the anguish of the Cross to the bliss of Paradise: "Father, into Thy hands I commend My spirit" (23:46).

Of our Lord's soul we read in Matthew (and also in Mark) that in the loneliness of Gethsemane He said, "My soul is exceeding sorrowful, even unto death" (26:38), and in John that as the last week of His path brought Him into the deepening shadows of the Cross, He said: "Now is My soul troubled, and what shall I say? Father, save Me from this hour: but for this cause came I unto this hour" (12:27). When Peter gave to the nation of Israel his triumphant word at Pentecost touching the risen and exalted Jesus, he appealed to the resurrection as being the fulfillment of David's prophecy, that "His soul was not left in hell, neither His flesh did see corruption" (Acts 2:31).

The witness to the reality of Christ's body is ample, from His birth of a virgin mother to His burial in a garden tomb.

To the Jews in Jerusalem in the beginning of His ministry He gave the supreme sign of His authority: "Destroy this temple, and in three days I will raise it up....But He spake of the temple of His body" (Jn. 2:18-21). Upon His body Mary poured her spikenard in preparation for His burial (Mt. 26:12). In the Upper Room the Lord gave the broken bread to the eleven, saying: "This is My body which is given for you" (Lk. 22:19). Finally, each Gospel relates how Joseph went to Pilate and begged the body of Jesus.

Beyond many such express references, there is a wealth of the record concerning the experiences of that holy body, and indeed of the whole of Christ's humanity. In infancy He was nursed and tended by His mother (Lk. 2:7), was presented to the Lord at forty days (Lk. 2:22; Lev. 12:1-8), and was taken up in the arms of the devout Simeon (Lk. 2:28). In His youth, He was subject to Joseph and Mary (Lk. 2:51), and exhibited a steady, healthful development of mind and body. We read that "Jesus increased in wisdom and stature, and in favour with God and man" (Lk. 2:52). As His path on earth began with birth, and hence He was first the infant, and then the child and the youth, so in each of these periods of life, He showed such mental and moral powers as were appropriate thereto.

That He increased in favour with God did not mean that God was at any moment other than well pleased with Him. Rather, it proclaimed that each successive stage, with its wider employment of faculties, and its greater experience of life, drew forth a corresponding pleasure on the part of God. Similarly, that He increased in wisdom did not mean that His wisdom was at any time at fault. Indeed, we read that as a child, He was filled with wisdom (Lk. 2:40). Rather does this increase in wisdom show that His consciousness developed in its powers in suitability to each stage of physical growth, even as the bud unfolds to the flower and each is perfect in its place. Yet in the mystery of His Person nothing of this detracted in any way from His constant possession of the fulness of Deity. Even at the age of twelve He could speak in true knowledge of His filial relationship with God (Lk. 2:49).

Testimony as to the reality of His consciousness in manhood as distinct from the omniscience of His Deity is borne by His own words touching the time of His coming in power and glory: "But of that day and that hour knoweth no man, no, not the angels which are in heaven, neither the Son, but the Father" (Mk. 13:32). It is noticeable that this passage occurs in Mark, the Gospel which particularly portrays Him in His servant character. It was in accord with the humility and the voluntary subjection to God that He displayed as the servant of God that He should will that in this one case, the date of the Advent, His divine knowledge should not be exercised in manhood consciousness during His abasement on earth.

From His Deity nothing was hidden, nor could be. On the other hand, the time of the advent was not part of that illumination divinely given to His human spirit. That such conditions should belong together to the One Person was not inconsistent with the mystery of His incarnation, but was akin to His possession of omnipresence in virtue of His Godhead, and of locality of presence in one place in virtue of His manhood.

In His ministry He was seen in weariness, after much toil, sitting on a well at Sychar, and sleeping in a ship on the Sea of Galilee. He was hungry when He fasted in the wilderness of the temptation, and when some days before His death He sought refreshment from the fig tree. Usually, however, He shared the ordinary food of His people. At His kingly entry into Jerusalem, He wept as He considered the coming destruction of the guilty city, and in Gethsemane

He sought comfort from His three disciples, saying to them: "Tarry ye here, and watch with Me" (Mt. 26:38). At Cana, He showed that He could rejoice with the friends gathered at the wedding feast, delighting in their day of gladness, and setting His approval upon it. Little children nestled in His arms. The homes of Martha and Zacchaeus and others made Him a most welcome guest, and found Him a loving and compassionate friend. In these and many other things, the Lord Jesus displayed a true manhood, marked by the features normal to the daily life of men, yet always apart from sin.

To our Lord's humanity there nevertheless was attached unique and transcendent dignity. In Him alone do we behold the perfection of manhood. Throughout the history of our race there have been those who by God's enablement have shown outstanding traits of nobility, of goodness and of grace. We speak of the purity of Joseph, the meekness of Moses, the patience of Job, the wisdom of Solomon, the devotion of Mary of Magdala, and the sacrificial love of Paul. But all such qualities are gathered up finally and completely in one glorious harmony in the Son of Man.

Indeed, it is in this title that the supremacy of His manhood is most set before us. Repeatedly the Lord spoke of Himself as the Son of Man, but only on three occasions, and those all in reference to His glorified state, did His people use the expression of Him (See Acts 7:56; Rev. 1:13; 14:14). Certainly it was Messianic, for Daniel writes: "One like the Son of Man came with the clouds of heaven...and there was given Him dominion, and glory, and a kingdom" (7:13-14). This the Lord claimed for Himself when He said to the disciples: "The tribes of the earth...shall see the Son of Man coming in the clouds of heaven with power and great glory" (Mt. 24:30). To Caiaphas He said: "Hereafter shall ye see the Son of Man sitting on the right hand of power, and coming in the clouds of heaven" (Mt. 26:64). Yet the Lord's use of the title in the Gospels shows its true meaning. It is more than an expression of His Messiahship; it is an assertion of His right—because of His character—to that very office.

That the Lord claimed for Himself such majesty of manhood is suggested by such a statement as "The foxes have holes, and the birds of the air have nests; but the Son of Man hath not where to lay His head" (Mt. 8:20). The beasts and the birds found a dwelling place, but He, the noblest to live on this earth, was a homeless stranger. Because He was the Son of Man, He had power on earth to forgive sins (Mk. 2:10), and authority was given to Him to execute judgment (Jn. 5:27). On one hand, Christ's dignity as the Son of Man showed the baseness of the betrayer and his treacherous kiss (Lk. 22:48); on the other hand, it looked to glorification as the true goal of His path (Jn. 12:23).

To our Lord, then, belonged humanity in the absolute sense. He embraced its every dignity so that in Him, and in Him alone, we see in its completeness the divine ideal of manhood. No excellence of character could be added to Him. There were no virtues for Him to acquire, for all were His at all times. In the garden of His soul there were no exotics; every fragrant plant was native to its setting.

In the perfection of His human spirit there was completeness of knowledge concerning the will of God. He alone among men could speak of what He would do on the morrow, saying: "I do cures today and tomorrow, and the third day I shall be perfected" (Lk. 13:32). For all others the word must be: "If the Lord will, we shall live, and do this, or that" (Jas. 4:15). No mistake was possible to Him, nor could there be necessity for any withdrawal or modification of any word from His lips. Hence He was not as Paul, who said: "I [knew] not, brethren, that he was the high priest" (Acts 23:5).

In the perfection of His soul there was the serenity of unbroken trust. When He saw that in the dispensation of God the wise and prudent did not perceive the things pertaining to Him, but that they were revealed to those of childlike faith, He answered: "Even so, Father: for so it seemed good in Thy sight" (Mt. 11:26). Thus He was not as Joseph, who, displeased with his father's act, showed his own frailty in the words: "Not so, my father" (Gen. 48:18). No doubt disturbed Christ's confidence in that which the Father had promised Him. Hence He was not as David, who, in spite of his anointing to kingship, said: "I shall now perish one day by the hand of Saul" (1 Sam. 27:1).

Though often weary, He was never despondent, but amid every trial manifested a stedfast assurance. Thus He was not as Elijah, who cast himself down under a juniper tree, and prayed that he might die (1 Ki. 19:4). Even to the death of the Cross He was obedient, breathing to the Father the prayer of infinite fragrance: "Nevertheless not My will, but Thine, be done" (Lk. 22:42). Thus He vindicated the Father's will before His apostles and His captors with the words: "The cup which My Father hath given Me, shall I not drink it?" (Jn. 18:11). He was not as Peter, who so objected to the truth of the Cross that he drew his sword and smote the high priest's servant (Jn. 18:10).

In the perfection of His body there was the vigour of superb health. His was a body prepared for Him of God (see Heb. 10:5), a body capable of pain and weariness but not of sickness, and capable of death but not subject to it. Being the body of the sinless Saviour, it could not know corruption either in life or in death. Corruption is the entail of the fall, and hence pertains to those who share that fall, but not to the holy One. Every faculty of Christ's holy body was thus free from impairment, and vindicated nobly the purpose of its being—doing the perfect will of God. Thus did He spend long days of incessant toil ministering to men, and long nights of prayer communing with God. Sometimes His hours of lovingkindness to hungry hearts were so full that they brought Him no opportunity to partake of bodily food (Mk. 3:20; 6:31). On one occasion He sat wearily on a well after a long journey on foot. But even in weariness, hunger, and thirst, He laboured on, refreshed by the joy of doing the Father's will (Jn. 4:34).

Possessing such glorious manhood, our Lord brought to His service no sense of inadequacy for the tasks before Him. Hence he was not as Moses and Jeremiah, pleading inability to speak God's message. Rather He said: "Lo, I come to do Thy will, O God" (Heb. 10:9). He stated: "I must work the works of Him that sent Me, while it is day" (Jn. 9:4); and again: "I do always those things that please Him" (Jn. 8:29). He was not as Isaiah, who, beholding the glory of the Holy One, was overcome with the sense of his own uncleanness of lips (Isa. 6:5), or as Daniel, whose comeliness was turned in him into corruption, and in whom there remained no strength, because he, too, saw the vision of the glorious One (Dan. 10:8).

These, with others of the noblest men of faith, were alike stricken with the fearful knowledge of their own unworthiness in the presence of God, but the Lord Jesus knew no such experience. In the pure light of God He lived, utterly at home in His presence, and enjoying without reserve the vision of His face. Thus was His path marked by service without sense of shortcoming, by obedience without hesitation, and by blessed activity of spirit, soul, and body that brought in its train no possibility of regret.

To the believing heart it is exquisite delight to contemplate the graces of Christ, and to learn from them the true meaning of manhood. The relationships of life are threefold—Godward, manward and selfward—and in each of these three spheres the Lord Jesus manifested Himself as the heavenly Man.

Godward: To the Jews who opposed Him He said: "Ye are from beneath; I am from above: ye are of this world; I am not of this world" (Jn. 8:23). Not only as to His eternity but as to His character He was from above. From this world He derived nothing; the spring of every attribute and trait, and of all their exercise, was God Himself. His were the words spoken through the prophet: "He wakeneth morning by morning, He wakeneth mine ear to hear as the learned" (Isa. 50:4), so that each new day He was wakened from sleep by the Father. Fresh and clear as the dew glistening in the stillness of the dawn, the first thoughts in His holy consciousness were of the Father and of the measureless wealth of His fatherhood love. Amid the incessant demands made on Him by the varied circumstances of the day, it was always the same. He lived by the Father (Jn. 6:57).

His was a life of implicit trust in the Father's care and of rest in the Father's will. On the angry lake He slept in peaceful repose; through the stormy scenes of passion and of pride that surrounded Him, He pursued His even way. When His own disciples were offended at Him, and drew back from the reproach of the Cross, He turned not back, but went on stedfastly, the unoffended Christ. In His heart was no restlessness of earth, but rather the calm of heaven; He was in heaven, and heaven in Him.

The purpose of manhood is fellowship with God, but even in Eden God was denied that which He sought. One Man alone gave Him all His heart's desire, and He the One whom God called "the Man that is My fellow" (Zech. 13:7). Nothing could mar this communion. It went on undiminished, not only in those hours and nights of prayer in the solitude of the hills, but in the busy days spent among the surging crowds. From His pure heart there could arise no earthborn cloud to hide from Him the sunshine of the Father's face. Walking with God in an intimacy which not even an Enoch could know, Christ gave heed in all things to the Word. It was precious to Him, and governed His life. To Him no commandment was grievous; each was fraught with perfect love. He stood before the high priest in silence while false witnesses spoke maliciously of Him. In this was fulfilled the saying: "As a sheep before her shearers is dumb, so He openeth not His mouth" (Isa. 53:7).

When the high priest adjured Him by the living God that He tell them whether He were the Son of God, He replied instantly: "Thou hast said" (Mt. 26:62-64). The Word had said that to hear the voice of adjuration and not to utter that which was seen or known was sin (Lev. 5:1, R.V.). Hence the sinless Christ opened His mouth and bore witness to His own Person. In silence and in speech, He was alike the perfect One who glorified the Word of the Lord.

The crown of His life of communion was the thanksgiving that rose up so gladly from His heart. Before He broke the loaves to the five thousand, He looked up to heaven and blessed them. When the seventy returned with joy from their mission, He said: "I thank Thee, O Father, Lord of heaven and earth, that Thou hast hid these things from the wise and prudent, and hast revealed them unto babes" (Lk. 10:21). At the tomb of Lazarus, He gave thanks to the Father before He spoke the word that raised the dead. When He instituted His Supper, He gave thanks for the bread and for the cup, in transcendent moral glory, blessing God for the body given Him in which to suffer His atoning death, and for the precious blood given Him to shed.

Before He went from the warmth of the upper room to the coldness of the lonely garden, a song of praise to God filled His holy lips. At Emmaus, He took the bread at the evening meal and blessed it before He broke and gave it to His friends. Amid joy and sorrow, He was the Man of praise, the music of whose thanksgiving shall be sweet to God's heart forever.

Manward: The Lord Jesus was utterly apart from those considerations of respect for creature pretension which so largely mold our attitude to other men. We are swayed by deference for social status, for worldly wealth, for beauty of form and elegance of dress. He did not look on these but on the character which in its innermost depths lay open to His view. With heavenly eyes beholding men, He appraised them according to their fear of the Lord (see Ps. 15:4), and delighted in the spiritual kinship which linked with Him those that did the will of God.

On one occasion, "He stretched forth His hand toward His disciples, and said: Behold My mother and My brethren! For whosoever shall do the will of My Father which is in heaven, the same is My brother, and sister, and mother" (Mt. 12:49-50). We are so blinded by our regard for fame and intellect and wealth that our proud hearts too often scorn those whom we call the degraded, the ignorant, and the homeless. The Pharisees derided the Lord Jesus because He received sinners and ate with them, but He looked on these outcasts with loving eyes that saw not only what they were but what they would be!

> *All around Him and beside Him,*
> *Sinners sat at meat—*
> *Sinful men and sinful women—*
> *Bread of heaven they eat.*
>
> *Only sinful men and women*
> *Men could see and scorn;*
> *He beheld them crowned with glory*
> *Of the heavenly morn.*

In this tireless love, the Son of Man gave Himself constantly to the needy hearts around Him. He accepted invitations to dine with Pharisees, yet stayed in the home of Martha of Bethany. To Nicodemus the ruler He gave a long interview, yet showed like grace to the despised Samaritan woman. He was most gentle with the frailty of sad hearts, and patient with the dulness of blighted lives: no lips were ever as kind as His, yet they could speak burning words when through them His righteous anger against the Pharisees for their hardness of heart poured white-hot from the fires of His holiness.

Being in such contact with the life that surged around Him, He entered with true sympathy into the sorrows which pressed on others' hearts. The Servant of Jehovah was indeed "a Man of sorrows, and acquainted with grief," even before He was uplifted on the Cross. He did not shun the cares of others, but sought out weary hearts that He might comfort them. With what joy did He restore to the grief-stricken widow of Nain her only son, and to the sorrowing parents of Capernaum their only daughter!

Even though our faculties are blurred by the corroding effect of our own sinfulness, yet if our minds could see at once all the care and pain in just one city, it would prove more than we could bear. Seeing that His compassions were exquisitely sensitive in their holy perfection, what, then, must have been the load which rested daily on the heart of the Saviour? Though the proud leaders of Israel despised His loving sympathy with the griefs of burdened ones, He pursued His path unchanged, manifesting a moral majesty to which they were strangers, and a glory of manhood to which history can offer no parallel.

Selfward: Our hearts have been so corrupted by their selfishness (that hideous idolatry) that it is only by divine grace that we can appreciate in any measure the beauty of the one heart that never knew this blight. "Men will praise thee," said the Psalmist, "when thou doest well to thyself" (Ps. 49:18). So truly is self-seeking a characteristic of our poor race! In refreshing contrast we behold the path of the Lord Jesus, and listen to the words that tell of its loveliness. "If I honour Myself, My honour is nothing: it is My Father that honoureth Me" (Jn. 8:54). "I receive not honour from men" (Jn. 5:41). "I am come in My Father's Name, and ye receive Me not: if another shall come in his own name, him ye will receive" (Jn. 5:43). "Even Christ pleased not Himself" (Rom. 15:3). "Christ glorified not Himself to be made an high priest" (Heb. 5:5).

Never once did the Lord Jesus seek fame for Himself. His was the mind in which, at His incarnation, He made Himself of no reputation, and such was His humility throughout His path. He sought no publicity for His miracles, nor did anything of the merely spectacular attach to them. Even the occasion of His Transfiguration was given Him of the Father; He would display the rightful glory of His Person only as pleased the Father. When He looked down the course of the centuries, and spoke to weary hearts His blessed words of invitation: "Come unto Me, all ye that labour and are heavy laden, and I will give you rest" (Mt. 11:28), there was no self-seeking in his heart. So it was when He said: "If any man thirst, let him come unto Me, and drink" (Jn. 7:37). Though He displayed Himself as the only source of rest and refreshment to the human heart, and attracted many to Himself, it was never of selfish motive, but for the Father's glory and their eternal good.

When He presented Himself as the giver of rest, He said: "Take My yoke upon you, and learn of Me; for I am meek and lowly in heart" (Mt. 11:29). Here is the secret of His character selfward, and of the mind which sought no personal honour. "I am meek and lowly in heart." No one else could have spoken such words. Moses, the meekest among men, would not have dared to use them; he would have felt instead his own unworthiness. Nor can we find other lips on which they would be true without qualification.

Meekness is not lack of strength, but rather the presence of it in control, the strength of character to accept the will of God in its entirety—without question, without dispute, and without resentment.

Lowliness is the recognition of man's true place before God, a place of humility befitting him even apart from the Fall; in Christ it was the grace in which He, though Lord of all, lived on earth in the acceptance of that complete dependence on God which belongs properly to humanity. The Son of Man, and He alone, was essentially meek and lowly.

In the Person of our Lord Jesus Christ we behold the full glory of humanity, its God-given nobility, and its wealth of beauty and purity. Yet His was a manhood of toil and tears, and a path consummated in the death of the Cross. But the path to the Cross led onward to the Throne, and His toil and tears have won our hearts forever.

CHAPTER SEVEN

His Holiness

Thoughts of His sojourn in this vale of tears—
The tale of love unfolded in those years
Of sinless suffering, and patient grace,
I love again, and yet again to trace.   —Mary J. Walker

Nothing should bring more joy to the heart of the child of God than a glimpse of the worth of the Lord Jesus Christ. Whether we view Him in His character or in His work, we must say of Him: "He is altogether lovely." He is perfect both in Himself and in His ways with us. The Word from beginning to end speaks with a single voice and proclaims that in Him is neither flaw nor the possibility of it.

Among the truths which Scripture teaches concerning His Person is that of *His absolute sinlessness.* The noblest men who come before us on the sacred page are but saved sinners; the Lord Jesus stands alone in the stainless beauty of perfect Manhood. We feel conscious at once of the immeasurable gulf between His character and theirs.

> *What need*
> *To speak of Noah, and of Abraham,*
> *Of Moses, David, Hezekiah, Job,*
> *Who sometimes trailed their garments on the earth*
> *Though whiter now than snow? But here was One*
> *Faultless though compassed with infirmity,*
> *In human weakness sinless, who had stooped*
> *Lower than angelhood in might, but dwarfed*
> *In uncreated goodness infinite*

The loftiest seraphim; no stern recluse,
As His forerunner; but the Guest and Friend
Of all who sought Him, mingling with all life
To breathe His holiness on all. No film
Obscured His spotless lustre. From His lips
Truth limpid without error flowed. —E. H. Bickersteth

No one realized the sinlessness of Christ more than the men who were most in His company and who knew Him best. It is a notorious fact that those most intimate with us see aspects of our character not so obvious to the casual acquaintance. Our standards of behaviour in public life may be sharply at variance with those shown in the seclusion of the home circle.

Such men as Peter and John were admitted to closest association with the Lord Jesus. They were the friends of His own choice, and companied with Him, not only amid the acclamation of the multitudes, but also when He tasted deeply of rejection and scorn. They saw Him under the fierce light of many a trying circumstance, and by their own pride and ambition added to the burden on His heart. They were with Him when He poured out His prayers to God, and saw Him weary and homeless. They beheld Him surrounded with hatred and ignominy, assailed with cruel lies regarding His birth, and derided for His teaching.

Nevertheless their testimony is explicit. Peter said concerning himself: "Depart from me; for I am a sinful man, O Lord" (Lk. 5:8). but of Christ he said: He "did no sin, neither was guile found in His mouth...Christ also hath once suffered for sins, the Just for the unjust" (1 Pet. 2:22; 3:18).

Nor is John less emphatic when he affirms: "If we say...we have no sin, we deceive ourselves, and the truth is not in us," but that Christ "was manifested to take away our sins; and in Him is no sin" (1 Jn. 1:8; 3:5).

To this we may add the clear witness of Paul, who suffered so much for His sake, and who so often met the bitter and relentless criticism of Jewish controversialists: "He hath made Him to be sin for us, who knew no sin; that we might be made the righteousness of God in Him" (2 Cor. 5:21). When Paul will set before us the life that truly befits the child of God, he tells us that "the truth is in Jesus" (Eph. 4:21), so that every mark of moral worth and everything which God prizes as being in accord with His own character, dwells fully in Him.

The ministry of the Lord Jesus was marked by stupendous claims. He offered rest to every burdened heart that would come to Him. He stated that if He were lifted up, He would draw all men unto Him, and that His voice would be heard and obeyed in every tomb. Beyond this, He asserted both His Deity and His eternity in terms which His foes could not mistake (see Jn. 5:18; 8:58-59). He did not claim merely to be good, but to be God. He did not speak as One excelling among men, but as being Himself the absolute standard of all purity and truth.

His statements were either true in their completeness or the grossest imposture; in these matters there could be no middle path. One proven flaw would have been sufficient to end His claims. Yet He openly challenged His enemies: "Which of you convinceth Me of sin?" (Jn. 8:46). Far from the challenge being taken up, it was vindicated from unexpected quarters. The chief priests met great difficulty in seeking a coherent tale with which to accuse Him (see Mt. 26:59-60). The Roman governor attempted to wash his hands of his responsibility, saying: "I am innocent of the blood of this just person" (Mt. 27:24). At His trial no voice was raised on His behalf, but in his death God gave Him two witnesses to attest to His character—a dying thief and a Roman centurion (Lk. 23:41, 47).

It is not only sinlessness that is affirmed of our Lord in Scripture; He is presented to us throughout the Word in the beauty of holiness. Long before His birth, the seraphim adored Him, crying: "Holy, Holy, Holy is the Lord of hosts" (Isa. 6:3). When Gabriel announced His coming birth to Mary, he said: "The Holy Ghost shall come upon thee, and the power of the Highest shall overshadow thee: therefore also that holy thing which shall be born of thee shall be called the Son of God" (Lk. 1:35).

It was by the power of the Holy Spirit that Christ was born of Mary; it was by the same power that He walked on earth in the surpassing beauty of His moral perfection. At Jordan, "the Holy Spirit descended in a bodily shape like a dove upon Him" (Lk. 3:22). To the temptation in the wilderness He went "full of the Holy Spirit" (Lk. 4:1). "In the power of the Spirit" He returned to Galilee and taught in the synagogues (Lk. 4:14).

From His birth to His death, He lived by the energy of the Holy Spirit so that the glory of His Manhood was indissolubly linked with the measureless fulness of the One who was the Spirit of the Father and yet the Spirit of the Son. Thus Christ served, till at last He "through the eternal Spirit offered Himself without spot to God" (Heb. 9:14). Peter took up the prophecy of David concerning Him: "Thou wilt not suffer Thine holy One to see corruption" (Acts 2:27). The prayers of the believers spoke of Him as "Thy holy Servant Jesus" (Acts 4:27, R.V.). Again, we read that: "such an High Priest became us, who is holy, harmless, undefiled, separate from sinners" (Heb. 7:26).

Holiness is far more than the absence of sin, for God was holy before there ever was a sin in the universe. It is positive virtue; it is completeness of character where every faculty is in perfect expression and in perfect accord; it is an infinite and glowing purity which has neither room for sin nor interest in it. Our Lord was perfect in holiness in every domain of His being. Where holiness was, sin could not be, for holiness and sin are mutually exclusive. Nothing could be added to that character which was always full of the love of righteousness and the hatred of iniquity.

Our Lord Jesus could not sin. We may not attribute to Him either sin or the possibility of it. From such a dishonour to His blessed Person the spiritual mind will recoil with horror. He was essentially the Holy One. When He became incarnate, He was still the Word, and hence unchanged as to His personality. The taking of humanity into union with Deity involved no subtraction from the fulness of His Person. Seeing that on earth, even in the depths of His humiliation, He was the everlasting God, it follows that *a peccable Christ would mean a peccable God.*

Moreover, His was a manhood prepared for Him. His human nature was in entire harmony with His divine nature, so that His taking it meant addition of experience, not variation of character. Holy humanity was united to Deity in one indivisible Person, the impeccable Christ.

He was "a Man of sorrows, and acquainted with grief." The experiences proper to holy manhood were His, so that He "was in all points tempted like as we are, yet without sin" (Heb. 4:15). The expression "like as we are" is that which is used in the same epistle: "after the similitude of Melchisedec" (Heb. 7:15). Our Lord was tempted in all points "after similitude (or likeness)," and the context would indicate that it was "after our likeness."

The limiting phrase "without sin" is joined not to "in all points," but to "after (our) likeness." Insofar as He was after our likeness, He was in all points tempted, but this likeness had one exception or limitation, it was without sin. It was not merely that temptation had no sequence of sin in our Lord Jesus, but that it found in Him neither sin nor occasion of it. We know, both from the Word and from our own sad experience, that when we are solicited to evil, within us are those cravings which are ready to respond to the tempter, and over which there is victory only by the power of the indwelling Holy Spirit. In Christ the Holy One such cravings never existed. There was nothing in Him to which any base suggestion might appeal; no breath of pollution ever rested on His holy mind.

"How then," it may be asked, "could He be tempted, seeing that He could not sin?" To answer this question which arises in the minds of many, we must notice the meaning of the word "tempt" in Scripture. It does not involve primarily any solicitation to sin, but refers to trying, testing, or proving. This may be illustrated by the following passages: "This He said to *prove* him; for He Himself knew what He would do" (Jn. 6:6). Christ's question to Philip tested him, but could not have any evil intent. *"Examine* yourselves, whether ye be in the faith" (2 Cor. 13:5). Here there is no thought whatever of sin. "By faith Abraham, when he was *tried,* offered up Isaac" (Heb. 11:17). Here Abraham was tested by God, in view of the glorious sequence to his faith. God tests for man's good, desiring only his blessing.

The additional element attaching to the word "tempt" may be ascribed to two factors. On the one hand, the devil tests also, but with evil motive, desiring only man's hurt. On the other hand, "God cannot be tempted with evil, neither tempteth He any man; but every man is tempted when he is drawn away of his own lust, and enticed" (Jas. 1:13-14).

Here, then, is the secret of our own tragedy—the presence in us of sinful tendencies, the desires of a fallen nature. In the Holy One of God there were never such tendencies, only the intensity of infinite purity. In us so often there is inward struggle against the entreaties of evil. We know the latter are wrong, but find in ourselves a deep-rooted sympathy toward them. In the Lord Jesus there was neither this sympathy nor this struggle. To His holiness sin was only repulsive, and hence it occasioned in Him no exercise as to whether He should respond to it.

It has been objected that because in our Lord's temptation the issue was not in doubt, the temptation was therefore an unreal one. This objection is merely superficial. The temptation was a proving of His character. That it proved it to be altogether holy did not indicate that there was any unreality in the malicious attack of the enemy. The temptation was most real, and its resultant suffering, with which we deal later, showed the intensity of the assault made on Him.

Again, it is objected that true manhood involves freedom of moral choice. This is true, but it does not imply any necessity for exercising that choice in a wrong way.

God Himself is a God of eternal liberty; He chooses what He pleases; nevertheless what He pleases is always right. Adam, given power of choice, chose that which was contrary to everything he knew of the God who had shown him only goodness. Though at the time he was unfallen he was without the experience of sin, yet he was not that holy thing. Adam prior to the Fall was sinless, but Christ was unchangeably holy. Christ's true manhood did indeed involve freedom of choice, but it was the unfettered choice of perfect holiness. Holiness chooses that which is holy; it is never untrue to itself. It cannot choose sin.

The temptation in the wilderness had two sides. Not only was there Satanic attack, but the Spirit of God led Christ to the scene (Mt. 4:1). The purpose of the Spirit could only be that our Lord should be proved. Not that there was any possibility of doubt as to the outcome, but that the perfection of His holiness should be displayed. As narrated in the

Gospel of Luke, which brings before us so prominently the humanity of Christ, the order of the three temptations was that of body, soul, and spirit, the three spheres of manhood. In each case, the tempter's suggestion was in essence that Christ should act independently of God.

In the first case, holiness refused the challenge to provide bread for bodily needs by the exercise of His power when there was no word from God so to do. In the second, holiness refused to give to a creature honour due only to God, and to receive kingship from other than the God who had promised it to Him already. In the third, holiness refused to make a trial of God's faithfulness for which there was no reason in the path of God's will.

In all these, and in the manifold temptations which surrounded His path, the Lord Jesus manifested unalloyed purity, and perfect dependence on the will of God. On Him was focused the glaring light of relentless opposition and bitter hatred, but no fault was ever discernible in Him. On the Cross, the indignity of men brought only the "Father, forgive them" from His lips.

Nor did His words and deeds ever suggest any resentment for the sorrows of His path. He was tried by the hunger, thirst and weariness which He was willing to experience, and by the anguish and pain of the shameful tree. He was tried by the callous mockery of the Roman soldiers, and by the derision of the frenzied mob that called for His crucifixion and then taunted Him on the Cross. He was tried deeply by the rejection meted out to Him by many to whom He had extended lovingkindness so freely. But whatever the trials, however sustained their duration, and however acute the suffering which they brought Him, they could only add their eloquent witness to the purity of His heart, and to the beauty of His ways.

"He Himself hath suffered being tempted" (Heb. 2:18).

He did suffer, not only in such circumstances as hunger and grief, but even when the enemy placed before Him those base suggestions to which there could be no possibility or His yielding. They caused Him deep pain, and that because of His very holiness.

If a Christian lady was suddenly taken from the atmosphere of a pure and sweet home, and made to reside among the unspeakable degradations of the slums of a great city, to listen to the coarse words and foul jibes on every hand, would she not suffer acutely from the sounds and sights so repellent to her? Do we not suffer when we hear the Name that is most dear to our hearts blasphemed either wantonly or by studied insult? If these things are true of us—in all our frailty and failure, in all our slowness to understand the glory of our God, and the exceeding sinfulness of sin—how must the Lord Jesus have suffered in the circumstances in which we are contemplating Him.

To His holy mind, with its exquisite sensibility, and with its measureless appreciation of the character of God, it entailed suffering to behold the repulsiveness of sin in the lives of the men and women who thronged around Him. And it was suffering beyond our comprehension that the evil one would suggest that He should act independently of God, and thus dishonour the Father in the fulness of whose love He had ever dwelt. Thus the very holiness which made it impossible for Him to sin brought Him intense suffering in temptation.

"But," it is asked again, "did not the Lord Jesus give us a perfect example as to our behaviour when assaulted by the foe?" To this further objection a twofold answer is necessary. First, if it is a matter of showing us the blessedness of calm repose on the Word of our God, then He gave us a true example. His was a path of undeviating obedience to the Scriptures. To Him they were all divinely authoritative;

in them He trusted with entire confidence. From Him we learn as from no one else how reverently we ought to receive the Word, how completely we should recognize it as given by God Himself

Secondly, if it is a matter of any struggle against yielding to evil suggestions, there was no sense in which Christ could be our example, for as we have seen, there was never any such struggle in Him. Our deliverance in the inward conflict between good and evil is not by His life but by His death, not by His example but by His Cross. There "our old man is crucified with Him...that henceforth we should not serve sin" (Rom. 6:6). We triumph only as we reckon ourselves "dead indeed unto sin, but alive unto God through Jesus Christ our Lord" (Rom. 6:11), and as we "through the Spirit do mortify the deeds of the body" (Rom. 8:13).

In all these things let us seek grace from God, lest we dishonour our beloved Lord by unworthy views of His character. Let us beware of thoughts that would seek to degrade to our level, we who are members of a fallen race, the One whose solitary perfection we have been contemplating. Let us listen afresh to the "Holy, Holy, Holy" of the seraphim, and remember that such as He was in their praises, He was still in His earthly path, and shall be forever.

CHAPTER EIGHT

His Transfiguration

In the Son there dwells all the fulness of absolute Godhead; they were no mere rays of Divine glory which gilded Him, lighting up His Person for a season and with a splendour not His own; but He was, and is, absolute and perfect God.   —R. C. Trench

Immanuel came to His own land, but for Him the nation had no royal welcome. Thus the feet of the One who had trodden the sapphire glories of heaven (Ex. 24:10) now toiled onward to the Cross. Steps of love they traced, steps on which the Father gazed with infinite delight. And when the Son began to witness concerning His sufferings (Mt. 16:21), the Father witnessed concerning His glory (2 Pet. 1:17). Wonderful was that foretaste when the awesome splendour, veiled since Bethlehem beneath the lowliness of His humanity, shone forth undiminished, and God's King was revealed in His beauty.

Previously, the god of this world from a high mountain had shown Him the kingdoms of this world and the glory of them (Mt. 4:8). The tempter's suggestion had found no response from the Holy One, and on another high mountain the God of heaven revealed the kingdom of heaven and its power. Yes, and its glory, too, the glory that belonged to the only One who was able and worthy to bear it.

The transfiguration was a glimpse of "the power and coming of our Lord Jesus Christ," as seen by those who "were eyewitnesses of His majesty" (2 Pet. 1:16). This is borne out by the words of the Lord Himself as narrated in the first three Gospels; words whose reference is obviously to the holy mount: "Verily I say unto you, There be some standing here, which shall not taste of death, till they see the Son of Man coming in His kingdom" (Mt. 16:28).

As befitting the Gospel which so much stresses Christ's kingship, the record in Matthew tells that the kingdom will be that of the Son of Man. It was after six days that Peter, James and John were taken into the high mountain to behold His glory, for it will be after the long, sad week of this world's sorrow and misrule that the righteous reign of the Son of Man will bring to earth its sabbath of millennial rest.

In Mark, the Gospel of the devoted Servant of God, obedient unto the Cross, the quotation is: "the kingdom of God come with power" (Mk. 9:1). The Servant claims not the kingdom for Himself; it is God's, but in the hands of the exalted Christ it will nevertheless come with power. Here, too, the bringing in of God's kingdom with power relates to the setting up of the thousand years' rule which shall bring to an end the power of rebellious men.

In Luke, the Gospel of the holy manhood, there occurs a further variation in the narrative. Here the words are simply "till they see the kingdom of God" (Lk. 9:27), but they are followed by the statement that "about an eight days after these sayings, He took Peter and John and James, and went up into a mountain to pray." The expression "about an eight days after," with its designed indefiniteness, points to the transfiguration as having taken place the seventh day after Christ's words, but shows that the aspect of the kingdom in view is not that of its introduction in power to give earth its sabbath, but of its duration into the eighth day of eternal peace, into a new heaven and a new earth.

Not in Jerusalem, nor even in Judaea, but away north of Galilee, the Lord took three of His own into a high moun-

tain apart (Mt. 17:1), and indeed it is always in the place
apart that His glory is revealed to the soul, where He
becomes to us a transfigured Christ. There on the mountain
height He prayed, for His was a life of unbroken dependence on God. His prayer is not told to us, but we do know
that as He prayed, His Person was suddenly radiant with
uncreated splendour. And what splendour it was! The
weariness of the mountain climb was lost in the vigour of
eternal days, and the derision of earth was hushed in the
salute from the excellent glory. The very mountain that lifted itself far above the clamour and sordidness of the life
that teemed around its base, was mute witness to His
excelling brightness.

Peter, looking back across the years, wrote that "He
received from God the Father honour and glory, when there
came such a voice to Him from the excellent glory, This is
My beloved Son, in whom I am well pleased" (2 Pet. 1:17).
Thus did the Father display His delight in that lowly One,
and proclaim Him as the Man His fellow. Thus did He bear
testimony to His Son in relation to the heavenly character
of His humanity, and His flawless fitness for the sacrificial
work of Calvary.

His blessed face shone as the sun (Mt. 17:2). As the
glowing orb in the skies gives to our earth its energy,
warmth, and light, so Christ is the sun of the universe. In
omnipotence He pours forth creative and upholding might,
bringing all things into existence and maintaining the succession of the ages. The voice that later aroused the
amazed disciples with its word of peace, "Arise," was the
voice that had spoken when the worlds had been framed. It
still spoke and by it all things were upheld.

In his vision in Patmos, John saw that "His countenance
was as the sun shineth in its strength" (Rev. 1:16), so that
the glorified Lord is the true sun in His church's sky, the

source of all power for overcoming, and of all warmth of love and cheer amid the wintry winds of time.

Seeing that the glory of the mount was peculiarly that of the coming kingdom, we recall God's message through the last of the Old Testament prophets: "Unto you that fear My Name shall the Sun of righteousness arise with healing in His wings" (Mal. 4:2). As the sun may be seen in the early morning, throwing from its fiery disc great shafts of light to the north and to the south as if extending a comforting embrace after the chill of night, so will the King appear to weary Israel and the nations, spreading His wings of love where once earth's darkest gloom held sway.

Once more we read of that resplendent countenance, this time at the Great White Throne (Rev. 20:11). There the blaze of Deity will so stream from His face as He sits as judge that the earth and the heaven will flee away, unable to bear such dread majesty.

Befitting His Person was the wonder of His garments. Matthew, in accordance with his description of the shining of the Lord's face, tells us that "His raiment was white as the light" (Mt. 17:2). As the pure light of the sun is not one colour, but the perfect blend of the sevenfold beauty seen in the rainbow, so the Person of Christ embraces every excellence of Deity. Holiness and love, majesty and grace, wisdom, truth and power, all the infinities have their one centre in Him.

Mark, portraying the worth of Christ's service, states that "His garments became glistering exceeding white; so as no fuller on earth can whiten them" (Mk. 9:3, R.V.). Compared with His garments, even snow would be dull. Its soft flakes, falling in their virgin whiteness from the skies, would be all that nature could offer to display the lustre of purity, but He was nature's Lord. Nor could any toil of earth produce such wonder. Christ, and Christ alone, is the heavenly fuller who makes whiter than snow. And it is He whose robes of character were ever like this, who delights to make the soiled garments of our life and ways like His own.

Luke says that His raiment was glistering (Lk. 9:29), an expression indicating that it was ablaze with dazzling light whose gleams could be compared only with the intense brilliance of the lightning flash. Such radiance it was that fell on Saul of Tarsus, and his own testimony was that he could not see for the glory of that light (Acts 9:3; 22:11).

With the Lord in such glory there appeared two heavenly visitors whose conversation gave clear evidence as to the mind of heaven. In the realms of light one theme has entire pre-eminence, one work alone is proclaimed, and one Man alone is exalted. As the cross of Christ is the theme of Scripture, so is it the theme of heaven, and this was told forth on the mount as Moses and Elijah talked with Him concerning His decease which He should accomplish at Jerusalem. All honour must be His. The three disciples, awakened at last from the heaviness of sleep, saw His glory and the two men who stood with Him. Not the glory of the men, but His glory was seen, for that in which Moses and Elias appeared was derived. But the glory of Christ was intrinsic, shining forth from the depths of His illimitable Person. (See Lk. 9:30-32.)

The path of dependence on the Father which the Lord entered at His birth was one in which He would receive nothing except it were given Him from heaven (cf. Jn. 3:27). He would be transfigured only when the Father's time should come to give to Him honour and glory. Nevertheless, while the glory was thus conferred as to its occasion, it was intrinsic as to its nature. The Lord walked on earth in the changeless possession of full Deity with every associated attribute and power. His glory was veiled by His humiliation, but could not be taken from Him, nor did He divest Himself of any of its splendour. It shone out in His miracles and in His character.

When Peter said that he had been an eyewitness of His majesty, he used for "majesty" a term expressing pure greatness, the same word occurring in Luke 9:43 and translated, "mighty power." The mighty power or the majesty of God was thus a matter of awe to the throng that beheld the healing of the sick boy. Although that miracle took place when the transfiguration was over, the same majesty was still attached to the Lord as on the holy mount.

Clearly, then, the radiance that was displayed on the mount was always His. Again, the term "transfiguration" refers not to the dress but to the nature, not to that which is separable, but to that which is essential. The glory was that of His own Person. Necessarily restrained and pent in by the self-humbling of the incarnation, it was permitted to burst from the fulness within, to light up His holy body and even His raiment with the splendour of eternity.

"There talked with Him two men" (Lk. 9:30). So intimate, even if reverent, was their relationship to Him that they conversed with Him as those made to be at home in His presence. Their privilege would have been great if they had only been permitted to gaze on Him from afar, or to lie on their faces at His feet in speechless adoration. But they were admitted to the greater honour of standing and communing with Him without distance and without fear. So will it be when the redeemed are with their Lord at His coming. In the nearness of a fellowship which nothing will ever mar, they will go with Him step by step into the realization of all the Father's purposes for the ages to come.

They spoke of His decease (i.e., His exodus) which He should accomplish at Jerusalem, not only of His death of shame and of sin-bearing, but of His resurrection and its endless joy. Never did the Lord foretell His crucifixion without speaking also of His rising again. The two are linked indissolubly both in type and in reality. Well might Moses and Elijah talk of *His* exodus, of *His* journey through the waves of death to the song of resurrection, for the one had gone though the Red Sea and the other through Jordan, yet with the waters held back by divine power (Ex. 14:22; 2 Ki. 2:8). Over their Lord the waves would sweep in their awful fury, till their force was forever spent. His alone would be the desolate cry of forsakenness (Mt. 27:46); His alone would be the joyous music of the victorious song (cf. Ps. 21:1). His decease would be accomplished (or fulfilled) at Jerusalem.

The law and the prophets pointed alike to the sufferings and the triumph of the Crucified; their words must be fulfilled, and the shadow of the type find its substance in the Person of the Son of God. Seeing that types and their antitype cannot abide together, the two men who represented the law and the prophets stood with Christ in token that He was the theme of all their witness, but then "departed from Him" (Lk. 9:33).

This testimony of the law and the prophets was full of significance, but there still awaited the voice that would supremely attest the person of the transfigured Lord. The two visitors had gone, but there was One in whose bosom the only-begotten Son dwelt in the fulness of love and communion. He must speak, and His presence-cloud, His Shekinah, overshadowed all the place. It was no mountain mist which wrapped the scene—such held no terror for the three hardy fishermen—but a cloud which Matthew describes as bright, i.e., luminous, or full of light (Mt. 17:5). Such was its nature that the disciples feared as they entered it, as surely they must, had they reflected on its history. In ancient days this cloud had appeared in the tabernacle and temple (Ex. 40:34; 1 Ki. 8:10); afresh would it be seen when the King of glory should come to reign (Isa. 4:5; Ezek. 10:4 with 43:2-3; Rev. 10:1). But on the mount it descended in a foretaste of that time.

It was identified by Peter in his second epistle as "the excellent glory." The voice which the writers of the Gospels speak of as coming from the cloud, he describes as being from that glory, or "brought...by the majestic glory" (R.V. marg.). Moreover, he relates that the voice came from heaven (2 Pet. 1:17-18), as if in the cloud coming to the mount, heaven bent low to place its caress of welcome and joy on the beloved One, and to declare that He, the Son of Man, would be the ladder from earth to heaven, that this was the true fulfillment of the dream of Jacob and of the prophecy to Nathanael (Gen. 28:12; Jn. 1:51).

Hushed be our hearts as this voice speaks. Submissive be these wayward wills as we listen to its words: "This is My beloved Son, in whom *I* am well pleased." There never was, there never shall be a time when the Son is other than the joy of His Father's heart and the light of His Father's face. Dwelling in eternal love, which has ceaselessly embraced One alone as its Beloved, the Son has met with completest response every desire of the heart of God. This beloved One it is the Father's joy to proclaim, witnessing alike to the glory of His sonship, and to the repose of Their ineffable communion.

"Hear ye Him" (Mt. 17:5). The beloved Son is the eternal Word, not only speaking words of life, but being Himself the Word of Life. Thus He is both the messenger and the message of the heart of God, whether in grace to the needy or in judgment to the scornful. The testimony of Moses and Elijah, and of the Father Himself, is all concerning the Son. He is the Beginning and the End, and all the Way in between. In Him all fulness dwells, and therefore an inexhaustible supply for our every need. He is the mystery of God (Col. 2:2, R.V.), His hidden plan for the ages to come, the centre and circumference of all His ways.

Twice in the Lord's path, first at His baptism, and then at His transfiguration, these words were spoken by the Father: "This is My beloved Son." (See Mt. 3:13-17). In the one case, the Lord stood at the beginning of His ministry, and the salute to His sonship looked back over the quiet years at Nazareth, and back into the depths of eternity. All this was involved in the words: "In whom I am well pleased."

In the other, the Lord was in the third year of His ministry, about eight or nine months from His death, and the Father's words looked forward not only to His Cross, but beyond it to the Throne and the everlasting kingdom. Here the divine pleasure beheld all dominion exercised by the beloved One, and founded securely on the infinite value of His atoning work. The first salute acclaimed the Man so pure and lowly as the Son who had come from glory, and the second as the One who went to it. The first had in view His stoop to death, and hence most fittingly was heard by the river Jordan; the second looked to His ascent beyond death to the crown, and so was heard on a high mountain.

As the transfiguration looked to the sequences of the Cross, there is to be noted a fivefold contrast between the majesty of the holy mount and the humiliation of Calvary. On the mount, the Lord's face shone as the sun; on the Cross "His visage was so marred more than any man" (Isa. 52:14). In the one scene, His raiment was white as the light, exceeding white and glistering; in the other His garments were taken from Him by the soldiers, parted among them, and even made the subject of their gambling (Mt. 27:35). In His glory, there stood with Him two of the greatest of His servants, men of pre-eminent nobility in Old Testament history; in His shame there were crucified with

Him two criminals, who cast their scorn in His teeth, and concerning whom it was written that "He was numbered with the transgressors" (Mt. 27:44; Mk. 15:28). On the mount was the cloud of light, the cloud of the divine presence; at Calvary "from the sixth hour there was darkness over all the land unto the ninth hour" (Mt. 27:45), darkness whose intensity we shall never comprehend. From the cloud of light there came the voice of infinite pleasure; from the darkness that enveloped the Crucified there came His anguished cry of desolation: "Why hast Thou forsaken Me?" (Mt. 27:46). In both scenes we behold the same Christ. Well may we adore, as in the words of the hymn:

> *Thou countenance transcendent,*
> *Thou life-creating Sun*
> *To worlds on Thee dependent,*
> *Yet bruised and spit upon!*
> *O Lord, what Thee tormented*
> *Was our sins' heavy load;*
> *We had the debt augmented*
> *Which Thou didst pay in blood!*

We look back once more to the holy mount. At length the witness was completed. The cloud passed and the display of Christ's glory, too. On the ground lay prostrate with awe the three who had seen His majesty. To them He came with loving touch and words of cheer and lifted their eyes to His. He remained, their own beloved Lord, whether on the mount or on the plain below, "Jesus Christ the same yesterday, and today, and forever" (Heb. 13:8).

Now by faith we see Him glorified. Let us dwell with Him, that we may see nothing else for the glory of that light. Then when we behold Him as He is, we shall find our Lord "Himself the goal of glory, Revealer and Revealed."

CHAPTER NINE

His Crucifixion

Still, O soul! the sign and wonder
Of all ages see—
Christ, thy God, the King of glory,
On the Cross for thee. —G. Ter Steegen

Throughout the centuries, the wonder of the Cross has not ceased to cast its sweet influence on the souls of men and women. They have gazed awestruck, and with contrite loving hearts, till nothing else has seemed of value, and the Crucified has been all in all. To those who lived nearest to it, the Christians of the first century, the Cross spoke of the deepest shame, and of the worst that earth could mete out to a bruised and weary form. They braved the scorn and contempt of a cynical age. To the Jews, Christ crucified was a scandal, and to the Greeks utter folly, yet the Christians lived, and loved, and triumphed. In our own day, the Cross has still its shame and its offence. Nevertheless, our thoughts are drawn irresistibly to that which is so despised, and our hearts prove that

'Tis heaven to dwell beneath the gaze
Of Jesus crucified.

It is in the Cross of our Lord Jesus Christ that we learn supremely the character of God, and His grace to a rebel creation. There the glory of the Incarnate Word is seen shining in all its fulness, displaying the immensities of its holiness and love. Prostrate in the anguish of Gethsemane, standing amid the rejection of Gabbatha, and nailed to the tree of utmost suffering at Golgotha, the despised and weary Saviour remained all that He had ever been, passing from depth to deeper depth of sorrow in the moral majesty which had marked His every step. In the darkness of the tomb He was still the Lord; even there we may discern the glory that was His alone.

Entering Gethsemane with three of His apostles, the Lord Jesus bade them pray, and was Himself withdrawn from them about a stone's cast (Lk. 22:41). This latter phrase, used nowhere else in Scripture, portrayed vividly the distance from men at which the One found Himself who met death under the sentence of the law given through Moses. The Lord knelt at this distance from the disciples, the very spot where He bowed in anguish, bearing a silent witness to the place which He would know in His death. There He gazed on that which was to be His experience on the morrow, when He, the only Man to keep the law of God in its entirety, and the only One upon whom it could have no claim, would bear its curse.

The prayer of agony, so dread in its intensity that "His sweat was as it were great drops of blood falling down to the ground" (Lk. 22:44), witnessed both to His holiness and to His obedience. The cup of which He spoke was the cup of judgment which He would drain upon the Cross, a cup from which His redeemed people will never drink. It was not the prospect of the suffering to be meted out to Him by His creatures, but that which He would experience in the darkness at Calvary—that and that alone brought from His lips the words: "Father, if Thou be willing, remove this cup from Me: nevertheless, not My will, but Thine, be done" (Lk. 22:42).

Let it not be thought that there was even the semblance of a difference between the will of the Father and the will of the perfect Man. Here was holiness indeed, and anguish beyond all creature understanding as His holy soul contemplated what it would mean for Him to be made sin. Here, too, was obedience, such as God could receive from no other. Throughout His path He had walked in constant obedience to the Father. At its beginning He had said: "Lo, I come to do Thy will, O God" (Heb. 10:9). Here in the Garden the same obedience was manifested, as He gazed into the depths of the cup. So precious to the Father was the fragrance arising from the heart and lips of His Son that the token of His pleasure in His Beloved was immediately given. The signpost which leads into the wealth of Luke's Gospel is surely the record in its first chapter of the priest in the temple, to whom—at the time of incense—an angel of the Lord appeared to convey the divine approval of his petition. Thus in Luke 22, if we understand aright, we find that an angel appeared to the lowly Man of sorrows, strengthening Him and by his very coming showing the Father's delight in the prayer which rose as fragrant incense even from those depths of suffering.

At the time of His arrest, there are set three glorious scenes. First, see the majesty before which the captors fell to the ground and the meekness that bore the traitorous kiss. Secondly, behold the love that led the Shepherd to interpose Himself between the wolves and the sheep, and the patience that endured being forsaken by His own. Thirdly, see the power that healed Malchus and the filial devotion which vindicated the Father's will before Peter. Each of these in itself was a manifestation of His glory. Together they proclaimed that He went to Golgotha, not by compulsion of men, but in the calm dignity of that journey which led by way of the Cross to the everlasting Throne.

Before the leaders of Israel, the despised King stood robed with the mocking purple and crowned with the piercing thorn. Weary after the long night's infamy, and bruised

by the weight of the cruel scourge, He listened to the derision of His nation, and at last to the apostate cry: "We have
no king but Caesar." The chief priests had rejected Jesus as
Christ, but now, driven on by their bitter hatred and their
desire for His death, they abandoned all their ancient long-
ings for their Messiah, and proclaimed the hated Gentile as
their king. What grief this apostasy meant for the One who
had said: "O Jerusalem, Jerusalem...how often would I
have gathered thy children together...and ye would not!"
(Lk. 13:34).

Amid all the tumult and the pain, the Lord Jesus bore
Himself with a grace that made the thorny wreath a true
crown of victory. Far from being demeaned by the humiliation heaped upon Him, He wore the purple and the thorns
with regal dignity, being never more kingly than when His
kingship was most derided.

Then the journey led outside the city gate to the place of
the skull. The Son of God was uplifted between two male-
factors, there to taste of the utmost shame, there "to bear
our sins in His own body on the Tree." Yet neither the journey nor the nails could diminish the glory of His ways. The
gentleness with which He said to the women who bewailed
Him: "Daughters of Jerusalem, weep not for Me, but weep
for yourselves, and for your children" (Lk. 23:28), and the
grace of the cries from the Cross, showed Him to be the
same compassionate Lover of souls that He had always
been.

Never had such words been known from the lips of a
crucified man as were heard that morning when earth had
offered its most dire and awful insult to the majesty of
heaven: "Father, forgive them; for they know not what they
do." They woke from its deadly slumber the soul of the
dying thief; they have bidden the men and women of nineteen centuries to taste of a love whose depths they can

never fathom. So it was with those other words that gave answer of eternal peace to the petition: "Remember me," and those that commended the grief-stricken mother to the care of John. They shall not cease to tell His fame.

With that tireless compassion for men there was linked an unbroken trust in the God who had willed the Cross. Not even in the words of intensest woe from the darkness was there a single note of resentment. In that forsakenness, the cry of the Crucified rose from an anguish which Deity alone could comprehend, but the trust of that pure heart faltered not nor failed. To the sufferer, God was still His God. His "Why hast Thou forsaken Me?" searched all the infinite dimensions of that most profound of mysteries, but did not question the righteousness and truth of the ways of God. When all was accomplished, and the victorious "It is finished" had gone forth to the universe, the Lord Jesus gave to the Father the tribute of the last words that His suffering lips would speak, words that consummated all His confidence in the Father's care: "Father, into Thy hands I commend My Spirit."

It was essential to His sacrifice that He who should bear the curse of the divine law as a substitute for sinners should be without condemnation from that law in respect to His own character. At the beginning of His public ministry, the Lord went to John to be baptized of him in Jordan. To the Baptist it was strange indeed that the sinless One—in whom there could be neither confession nor repentance—should come to him with such purpose. Christ's baptism was unique. He entered the river that spoke of death as no one else could, in the beauty of intrinsic holiness. If, then, He was to be baptized, it was in grace in which He was linking Himself with His needy people. When at the end of that path of grace He entered *that other Jordan,* where the waters of His atoning death should roll in all their pitiless torrent over His head, it was in the perfection of that same holiness. He alone could enter death in the merit of His own character, nor could He avail as the Sin-Bearer on any other ground.

Peter, writing of our redemption, speaks of Christ as "a Lamb without blemish and without spot." If the sacrifice brought to a Jewish altar was perfect externally, it was pronounced "without spot." If later scrutiny displayed it to be perfect internally, it was said to be "without blemish." With such allusion does the apostle speak of his Lord. From every viewpoint He was the Lamb of God's own providing. The true sin-offering, His character was foreshadowed in the requirement of the Levitical ritual: "This is the law of the sin-offering: in the place where the burnt offering is killed, shall the sin offering be killed before the Lord: it is most holy" (Lev. 6:25). Our Saviour was most holy even when bearing our sins in His own body on the tree.

For three hours, darkness was over all the land. Remarkably, Scripture makes no mention of the reaction of any man or woman to that supernatural shroud, neither of priests, nor of soldiers, nor of the feeble few who, loving Christ, stood by His Cross. The Word of our God displays the wisdom of its Author in that which it conceals as well as in that which it reveals. Seeing that we are told nothing of what either friends or foes thought or said during those hours, we conclude that for us who now muse upon the darkness every sound has been hushed and every voice stilled that we might listen to one cry and one alone.

As that veil of night was lifting, the cry rose, single, echoless, in all its uniqueness: "My God, My God, why hast Thou forsaken Me?" It was the only key to the darkness, which otherwise would be an impenetrable mystery. Midst all that man could do, Christ spoke words of forgiveness and blessing, but that which He experienced in those three hours brought to His lips the cry of direst agony. So the darkness contained that in which man had no part. It was then that the Saviour endured the forsakenness—and that of His God—a forsakenness involved in His bearing our sins, and thus in the making of atonement. The latter was a work wrought entirely of God. Man had no share in it. His guilty hands might nail the Lord Jesus to the Cross, but more than that he could not do; he might add to his sins, but could do nothing for their removal. The supreme sufferings of Christ were not at creature hands. They were endured when "the Lord laid on Him the iniquity of us all."

> *The gloomy garden, blood bedewed,*
> *The hideous midnight's shame and scorn,*
> *The scourge, the wreath of rending thorn,*
> *The tortures of the dreadful Rood—*
> *These were the billows of Thy death,*
> *Its storm-tossed surface, but the cry*
> *The spirit's woe—Sabachthani—*
> *Rose from the ocean underneath.*

When all is of God, all is perfect grace. The wonder of grace is that, altogether apart from us, the Saviour so fulfilled the will of God that He rendered to Him a complete satisfaction for the sins of all who believe. This exceeding value of the death of Christ is available for all men, for all was done on their behalf, but only those who believe actually benefit by it. It lies at the very heart of the doctrine of the atonement that Christ satisfied every claim of God on account of our sins. Not only does sin besmirch the sinner, and corrupt all his being, but it calls forth the judgment of God. Otherwise God would not be God, and righteousness would be a mockery. The divine holiness demands the execution of its penalty on the sinner. There can be no salvation apart from the meeting of the claims of God's character, and apart from the sustaining of judgment. This judgment was endured for us by our Substitute. He died in our place, the guiltless for the guilty, as Scripture expressly witnesses. "Christ also hath once suffered for sins, the Just for the unjust, that He might bring us to God" (1 Pet. 3:18). When He took our place, there was no imputing to Him of personal guilt, but only of liability for our sins. The guilt was altogether ours; the enduring of judgment was altogether His. His love led Him to accept this liability, and to discharge it by His atoning death.

"For He hath made Him to be sin for us, who knew no sin; that we might be made the righteousness of God in Him" (2 Cor. 5:21). Our adorable Lord Jesus Christ was made sin. This is not a statement of character, for He remained infinitely holy. He knew no sin. But it does tell of the position into which He went for us. He was made sin in that when He bore our sins He was treated with the treatment accorded to sin, i.e., there was poured on Him the judgment of God.

Never in the study of the Word of God is there more need for deep reverence and for holy caution than when we ponder the mystery of the actual sufferings of Christ. Those who were witnesses of His agony impress us by their profound reticence to give description. Yet beyond all that they could see was that which was veiled in the darkness. No creature gaze beheld the pains that were Christ's when under the judgment. Only in the Godhead is it known (but there it is fully known) what the Holy One endured for us. We are in every sense dependent on divine revelation for all that has been told us concerning this sacred theme.

Indeed, it is to the prophecies of the Old Testament that we must look if our hearts are to muse aright on the Saviour's deep woe. In one of these writings, antedating the Crucifixion by seven centuries, we read: "His visage was so marred more than any man, and His form more than the sons of men" (Isa. 52:14). If language has meaning at all, these words surely tell us of something beyond all parallel. The earlier statement: "As many were astonied at Thee," is God's word of infinite tenderness to His own Servant (and the only part of that supreme Song of the Passion directly addressed to the Servant). It relates to men's bewildered gaze on the suffering Christ, but the words "marred more than any man" tell of what God alone could know. This was not as a result of the indignities inflicted by men, but from the enduring of the divine wrath spent upon Him as the Sin-Bearer. Can we consider these things with tearless eyes and with hearts unmoved? Shall we not bow before our Saviour with brokenness of spirit, and confess to Him:

> *The tempest's awful voice was heard;*
> *O Christ, it broke on Thee.*
> *Thine open bosom was my ward:*
> *It braved the storm for me:*
> *Thy form was scarred, Thy visage marred—*
> *Now cloudless peace for me.*

In the ritual of the sin-offering, the glory of Christ as the Sin-Bearer was strikingly typified. We have seen that this offering was most holy, but we note also that while the body of the slain animal was burnt outside the camp in a clean place, its fat and associated parts were burnt on the altar of burnt-offering (Lev. 4:10, 19, 26, 31, 35). In the place of judgment, the fire, which symbolized the holiness of God, consumed the body of the offering; on the altar of burnt-offering, it made manifest the sweet savour of the fat. God's outpoured judgment, and His enjoyment of the savour of rest, were thus simultaneous.

But what type could set forth adequately the fulness of the Antitype? At the Cross, the Holy One was made sin, and endured the judgment of God, but never was He more precious to the Father than at that very time. Though it is far beyond the ability of the finite mind to reconcile these two things, yet were they true together. The Son dwelt in the bosom of the Father, and was loved with everlasting love. Even in His deepest sorrow, there was neither impairment of that place in the bosom, nor cessation of that love. The very obedience unto death which was rendered by the Son was a source of exquisite joy to the Father. Yet was He forsaken of God, and made a curse for us.

Knowing all the sweetness of the Father's love, the Lord Jesus tasted also all the bitterness of the divine forsaking. Only that heart which had itself embraced the vast dimension of the one could fathom all the dread reality of the other. This our Saviour did. In the infinite fulness of His holy consciousness there was the capacity to experience at once the distance between such height of bliss and such depth of woe. In the darkness of Calvary that pure and loving heart knew both together. He was in the bosom, and yet the forsaken One. Therein we behold a majesty of Person, and an extremity of suffering both beyond all mortal understanding.

Great as was the suffering, however, it was exceeded by the love that bore it. The love of Christ that led Him to be the substitute for sinners exhausted the sufferings, but the sufferings could never exhaust the love. Nothing could frustrate its blessed purpose, or rob it of its chosen trophies. It remained in its infinite grandeur, and triumphed over every sorrow. "He was as infinite in His condescensions as in His majesty." How wonderful was then the love that dictated all!

At length there came the moment appointed by the Father when the Lord Jesus should lay down the life which no man could take from Him. In His dying, He displayed

His glory: His death was both voluntary and victorious; in His own might, He dismissed His Spirit. By reverent hands the holy body was taken from the Cross, and tenderly laid in Joseph's new tomb with every attention which loving hearts were able to bestow. But even in death He was still the Lord.

At the Incarnation, the eternal Word took to Himself—in a union whose bond could never be altered—all that pertained to humanity, in spirit, soul and body. Though in the dissolution of death, spirit and soul were separated from the body, yet the body on the one hand and the spirit and soul on the other were maintained in their inviolable bond with Deity.

The spirit and soul went forth into the disembodied state (for such is the simplest and the only necessary meaning of His entering Hades—see Acts 2:31), and in the pure beauty of holiness went up to the Father, to His paradise, to the heaven of heavens. The body was laid in the tomb. It could not see corruption, retaining, till the moment when it was taken up in the new dignity of resurrection, its perfect fitness to be the dwelling place of the soul.

After the Crucified had risen from the dead, Mary Magdalene "looked into the sepulchre, and seeth two angels in white sitting, the one at the head, and the other at the feet, where the body of Jesus had lain" (Jn. 20:12). What their thoughts were as they sat in that hallowed spot we have not been told, but this is certain, that with heavenly wisdom they appreciated the real worth of the One whom men rejected. Thus it was that one of the angels said: "Come, see the place where the Lord lay" (Mt. 28:6). Even while in the tomb, He was still the Lord, and still worthy of all love and adoration.

We contemplate the Person of our Lord and Saviour in the various scenes which pass before our thought. We see

Him in the years of His ministry, in the hours of His suffering on the Cross, in the days and nights between His dying and His rising again, and in the ages of His resurrection power. Beholding His glory, we salute Him adoringly as being in all of these, "God blessed forever."

CHAPTER TEN

His Exaltation

Our longing eyes would fain behold
That bright and blessed brow
Once wrung with bitterest anguish, wear
Its crown of glory now. —Sir Edward Denny

Resurrection: Through the first four thousand years of the history of our fallen race, death reigned with undisputed sway. Except for two, Enoch and Elijah, who were translated to heaven, none escaped its stern demand. Neither excellence of strength nor of character availed to withstand its dark dominion. Then all was changed on that first day of the week when the Son of God stepped from the tomb in the dignity of indissoluble life. His last humiliation over, there could be nothing for our Lord from that moment but increasing exaltation. His triumph was complete. Forever vanquished, "Death laid its sceptre at the Victor's feet."

To the beloved apostle on Patmos, the Lord drew near and spoke the words whose note of jubilation still rings in the hearts of His believing people. "Fear not; I am the first and the last, and the Living One; and I was dead, and behold, I am alive for evermore, and I have the keys of death and of Hades" (Rev. 1:17-18, R.V.). Here was victory such as Caesar's legions had never gained. The Lord who had power to lay down His life had power to take it again. He surrendered nothing to the grasp of death, but brought forth the marks of His accomplished passion to be the infallible proofs of His resurrection. As pierced hands and feet and riven side had witnessed to His humiliation, it was most fitting that they should attest to His glory, and proclaim Him both risen and triumphant. The body which had lain in the tomb He displayed in the fulness of its energies, so that He not only ate and drank with His disciples during the forty days before the ascension, but manifested Himself the same Lord of grace that they had known in the preceding years.

It was indeed the body in which He had borne our sins that the Lord Jesus possessed in resurrection. Nevertheless, a change had passed over it. Up till death, it had been "the body of His flesh" (Col. 1:22), and soon at the ascension it would be "the body of His glory" (Phil. 3:21, R.V.). When it was seen in risen life, there no longer pertained to it the weakness which the Lord had voluntarily accepted at His incarnation, i.e., that capacity for suffering and death which was necessary for the accomplishment of His purposes in life and on the Cross. No longer would it know weariness and hunger, be afflicted by anguish and pain, or taste of death. The conditions which obviously attached to it in resurrection gave evidence that its sphere was heaven rather than earth.

That it could be visible or invisible to mortal gaze, or that it could dispense with the usual way of entering a closed room, was not extraordinary to it, but that which characterized its new dignity. The contrast between the expression "flesh and blood" used of Christ in incarnation (see Heb. 2:14), and that used of Him after He rose from the dead, "flesh and bone" (Lk. 24:39), is surely not without its significance as indicating that the sustaining of the body's energy was no longer dependent on the activities of the blood stream, but was ministered to inscrutably from a higher source, i.e., from the omnipotent life dwelling so richly in Him.

Christ's moral majesty in resurrection was seen markedly in the first words to come from His lips in His new life. Were they expressive of His supreme victory, or of His own gladness as brought again from the dead? No, it was the joy of One who was able to do that which had been His purpose in all His path of suffering. Here was the first fulfillment of that promise whose completeness, whether personal or national, should span two thousand years. "He will swallow up death in victory; and the Lord God will wipe away tears from off all faces" (Isa. 25:8).

So it was that the first words of the Risen One were addressed to drying the tears of a brokenhearted woman (Jn. 20:15). Mary Magdalene loved her Lord as did few of the disciples. Lingering at the Cross till the last, and then beholding how the sacred body was placed in the tomb, she could not be content apart from the One who had set her free from bondage, and brought the peace of heaven to her soul. Even in death He was still most precious to her; He was still her Lord, as her words dearly showed: "They have taken away my Lord."

The grace of the Conqueror had two aspects. In the one question: "Why weepest thou?" He displayed His purpose to take away all cause of sorrow; and in the other: "Whom seekest thou?" He expressed His power to satisfy the believing life by granting all its desire.

All the appearances of the risen Lord had a dual meaning. He showed Himself alive, and He also prepared His own for His going to God's right hand. While He ended Mary's sadness, He pointed her onward to His ascension. Well He knew that what she craved was nearness to Him. But as she sought to retain Him as the One she had known in the years of His ministry, He gently refused her clasp, and looked on to the greater nearness which should be hers after He had sent down the Spirit from the Father. Had He stayed on earth, she might at the most have touched Him occasionally. When He went to heaven, she would be, from Pentecost and forever, a member of His mystical body, and thus part of Himself. This same twofold purpose was evident on that night when the Lord stood in the midst of His disciples and showed them His hands and His side. He was not only the victor over death, but the giver of life. In a gladness excelling all that Eden knew, He was the Adam of the wounded side, and yet the Lord God of the life-imparting breath (See Gen. 2:7, 21; Jn. 20:20-23).

In the words, "So send I you," He commissioned His own for their service when He should be withdrawn from their sight. In those words He spoke when He breathed on them, "Receive ye the Holy Ghost," He linked with His own risen Person the mighty fact to be realized at Pentecost when they should be empowered for that service. In those words concerning the remission of sins, He pointed to a major part of that service in bearing to men the only message that could tell how sins could be forgiven. "And so it is written, The first man Adam was made a living soul; the last Adam was made a quickening spirit" (1 Cor. 15:45).

The Lord's pre-eminence in resurrection is set forth in three aspects in the Word. To Agrippa, Paul declared Christ to be the first that should rise from the dead (Acts 26:23). Here was *priority in time*. Though the fact of resurrection had been plainly taught in the Old Testament, its land of joy and song was all untrodden till the pierced feet of the Son of God began their triumphal march from the tomb.

Writing to the Colossians, the apostle proclaimed Christ as the firstborn from the dead (Col. 1:18). Here was *priority also in rank*. As the Firstborn in relation to every creature, the Son was the heir and sovereign of all, but as Firstborn from the dead He acquired a new inheritance and a new sovereignty in respect to all who should share His victory over death. Whereas His place as Firstborn of every creature was a solitary one in virtue of the uniqueness of His Sonship, that which is His as Firstborn from the dead has linked with it the joy of a new relationship, for He shall yet be seen as the Firstborn among many brethren (Rom. 8:29). His risen life will be fully shared by His redeemed ones when they, too, have done with death.

Again, Paul wrote to the Corinthians: "Now is Christ risen from the dead, and become the firstfruits of them that slept" (1 Cor. 15:20). Here was *priority also of fruitfulness.* As in Israel, the firstfruits of the harvest were peculiarly God's portion, so was Christ in resurrection. These nineteen centuries God has enjoyed His firstfruits in the beloved One who was received from death and taken to His side, and who is the cause, the pledge, and the sample of the fulness of the harvest.

Ascension: "And He led them out as far as to Bethany, and He lifted up His hands, and blessed them. And it came to pass while He blessed them, He was parted from them, and carried up into heaven" (Lk. 24:50-51). Though the Lord Jesus had become dear to His disciples as no one else could ever be, not a tear was shed when He was parted from them. So truly did they realize the meaning of His ascension, and its sequences for Him and for them, that their hearts overflowed with exuberant joy.

The Lord's last act before He passed from their sight was to lift up His pierced hands in blessing. In that attitude He was carried up. The nailprints which had witnessed to the reality of His resurrection were to be the token that He was taking up into heaven the body which He had brought from death, and indeed that in returning to the high place from which He had come, He was relinquishing nothing of His humanity. Those precious engravings of eternal love were unmistakable evidence that His grace of manhood would abide unchanged amid the splendour of the Throne. All that

He had been in the beauty of His character, in faithfulness, in sympathy, in mercy, and in truth, He would be forever. As in His stoop from heaven to earth, He remained true God, so in His exaltation from earth to heaven, He remained true Man.

"He was carried up into heaven." "He ascended up far above all heavens" (Eph. 4:10). His going up must not be considered merely in relation to this rotating globe with its local directions of space, but in respect to the whole creation.

To that whole system which we call the universe, there must be an ultimate "above," and that is where the Throne is, that is where God manifests His glory and dominion. Our Lord's journey led upward beyond the stars, beyond the angels, beyond every sphere which the creature could know and still upward to the supreme heights of Godhead majesty. Christ ascended not only from earth with its dishonour and rejection till He was higher than the heavens, but upward from all the self-humbling of the days of His flesh to the transcendent glory which belonged solely to the everlasting God.

These two aspects of His exaltation—His relationship to His creatures, and to God Himself—are brought together in Ephesians 1:20-21. In regard to the first, God set Him "far above all principality, and power, and might, and dominion, and every name that is named, not only in this world, but also in that which is to come." In regard to the other, He set Him "at His own right hand."

The time is coming when the godly of Israel will recognise that He of whom Jehovah spoke as "the Man that is My Fellow" was none other than the despised "Man of sorrows." Then will they see in Him their one hope, and their prayer will be: "Let Thy hand be upon the Man of Thy right hand, upon the Son of Man whom Thou madest strong for

Thyself" (Ps. 80:17). He is marked out from all others as "the Man of God's right hand." This honour none can share with Him. The right hand is the place of majesty where the Lord Jesus exercises all the authority, and wields all the power of Deity. At the Incarnation, the Father entrusted Him with all redemption, and such was His delight in the lowly Man of Calvary that He lifted Him up exceedingly and entrusted Him with all dominion. For the Beloved One this sphere of exaltation is that of the welcome smile.

When the crucified and risen Lord entered the heaven of heavens, He was greeted with the joyous salute: "Sit on My right hand, until I make Thine enemies Thy footstool" (Heb. 1:13). There God made Him most blessed forever; there He made Him exceeding glad with His countenance (see Ps. 21:6). There the everlasting love which had never ceased to enfold Him in its glad embrace gave to Him all its desire, and all His desire, too. There, in the measureless bliss of the inner life of God, the One who tasted the uttermost sorrow is enwrapped for evermore.

In the prayer concerning His ascension, where He looked back over His finished work and forward to the time when His people should be with Him, the Lord said: "Now, O Father, glorify Thou Me with Thine own self with the glory which I had with Thee before the world was" (Jn. 17:5). In the complete answer which was given to this request, the Son went back to the splendour which had been eternally His. From one viewpoint, He could go no higher than He was before, and He was but re-assuming the rightful place which He had left but never abdicated.

Yet from another aspect, the glory was reward given Him by the Father, and it invested Him in a manner not known in His pre-existence. For now when He ascended, the Lord took His humanity. Though He retained the form of a servant, as indeed He ever shall, it was no longer to veil the form of God. Never again to be restrained by any humiliation, the splendour of Deity shone forth in its infinite fulness, and that through the pure manhood in which Christ had triumphed on the Cross.

This was revealed in the words spoken through the prophet: "Behold, My servant shall deal prudently, He shall be exalted and extolled, and be very high" (Isa. 52:13). The terms "exalted and extolled" were those used in the description of His pre-incarnation state in Isaiah 6:1, "high and lifted up," and those used of His eternity in Isaiah 57:15, "high and lofty," so that the promise was that the Servant should once again have His original glory. Moreover, in the wonder of that exaltation of the Sufferer whose "visage was marred more than any man, and His form more than the sons of men," there was added the sublime expression "very high," as if to show that new lustre accrued to His majesty by virtue of the triumphs of His death and resurrection.

It pleased God that there should be three eye-witnesses even in this mortal body, of the glory of the ascended Christ. It is recorded of Stephen, the first Christian martyr, that while he stood in the Jewish council, among men who gnashed on him with their teeth, "he, being full of the Holy Ghost, looked up stedfastly into heaven, and saw the glory of God, and Jesus standing on the right hand of God" (Acts 7:55). With that scene of glory open to his gaze, and with its reflection on his face, the martyr met death fearlessly and passed to be with Christ.

To Saul of Tarsus, whose life was linked so truly with that of Stephen, there came the supreme moment when, as he was travelling to Damascus, there shone from heaven a great light round about him (see Acts 22:6). Never did Paul describe what he beheld in that glory beam, except for such brief allusions as: "Have I not seen Jesus Christ our Lord?"

and "He was seen of me also" (I Cor. 9:1; 15:8). It is rather from those years of unwearied devotion and of manifold suffering that we learn what that sight was. The secret of Paul's life was his vision of the King in His beauty, and of the lovely face from which shone all the glory of God.

The third witness was John who, in the Spirit on the Lord's day, saw One like unto the Son of Man. The vision was more than the mortal frame could bear. Such was the overwhelming majesty revealed to the exile that he fell at his Lord's feet as dead. John saw that:

> *"His head and hairs were white like wool;*
> *His eyes a fiery flame,*
> *Not tearful now as when He trod*
> *This world of sin and shame,*
> *His countenance was as the sun,*
> *His voice was as the sound*
> *Of many waters, murmuring deep,*
> *In harmony profound.*

> *"And when before His feet, as dead,*
> *The loved disciple fell,*
> *How gently deigned the Prince of Life*
> *His servant's fears to quell!*
> *And give him strength to see His face,*
> *Whom highest heavens adore —*
> *The Lord, who "liveth, and was slain,"*
> *And lives for evermore!"*

As it was in grace that our Lord came to earth, so it was that He returned to heaven. He entered within the veil as the Forerunner (Heb. 6:1-20), as the One whose presence there would make certain that His people would follow where He had gone. It was fitting that the lesser should be the forerunner for the greater, as John the Baptist was for

Christ: "He that cometh after Me is mightier than I, whose shoes I am not worthy to bear" (Mt. 3:11). Nevertheless, the Almighty Conqueror went in for the sakes of those who believe in Him, that we—so unworthy—might find heaven a place prepared for us. That which made it such was His presence within the veil in glorified Manhood, and in all the acceptance in which He was welcomed as the One who had accomplished the work of atonement. When the Lord Jesus took His seat at God's right hand, all was prepared, and, while still on earth, His people could rejoice that the Father's house was their true home. While we wait for His coming, we see in Him, as the glorified Man, both the display and the certainty of that which we shall be. Thus on our homeward journey we delight to sing:

> *No future but glory, Lord Jesus, have we,*
> *For man is in glory, already, in Thee;*
> *The brighter the glory that shines on Thy face,*
> *The clearer our title to glory, through grace.*

Enthronement: "I also overcame, and am set down with My Father in His throne" (Rev. 3:21). The Cross was the appointed way by which Christ went to the Throne. The travail of His soul won for Him the crown of glory and honour which now adorns His brow. So complete was His work on earth, and so vast the reward to which He went that all the wreaths of victory to be worn by His people will simply be degrees of fellowship with Him in the honours that must be pre-eminently His. There can be no crowns for the victors which do not belong first to the mighty Victor Himself.

Our Lord's session on the Throne involves many glories and many functions of majesty. To Him belongs the name which is above every name. As His path of humiliation embraced three phases, so the answering exaltation had its three corresponding parts (see Phil. 2:5-11). The steps downward we may list as:

(a) "He thought it not robbery to be equal with God."

(b) "He made Himself of no reputation."

(c) "He humbled Himself."

The steps upward we may list to show the correspondence as:

(c) "God also hath highly exalted Him."

(b) "and given Him a name which is above every name."

(a) "that at the name of Jesus every knee should bow...and that every tongue should confess that Jesus Christ is Lord, to the glory of God the Father."

In the symmetry of the passage, the first step downward (a) is answered by the last upward *(a)*; the second downward (b) by the second upward *(b);* and the last downward (c) by the first upward *(c)*. Thus "He humbled Himself" is balanced by "God hath highly exalted Him"; "He made Himself of no reputation" is balanced by "given a name above every name"; "equal with God" (i.e., in circumstance and state) is balanced by "every knee bow...every tongue confess." It is noticeable that in the steps downward it is in each case the Lord's act that is set forth, and in those upward it is the Father's act.

As the tribute of His approval, the God who beautifies the meek with salvation gave to the obedient One the name above every name. This was reputation indeed. The name is not to be confused with any of its parts, such as Son, Lord and Christ; these are bright stars, but the name is the whole constellation. It is the sum of all His relationships, the index of a majesty which no creature can bear, whose heights none can measure. Similar to this fulness, with the name having many components, is that in Isaiah 9:6, "And His name shall be called Wonderful, Counsellor, the mighty God, the everlasting Father, the Prince of Peace."

At the name of Jesus every knee shall bow, and every tongue shall confess that Jesus Christ is Lord. This decree must be obeyed ultimately throughout the universe. To the Victor of Calvary every creature shall render homage, either by choice or by compulsion. To His redeemed ones it is a deep delight to bow before Him in worship. On many occasions during the Lord's life on earth, the disciples gave Him this honour, and when from the slopes of Olivet He was carried up into heaven, the first act of the company that saw Him ascend was to worship Him. Their worship followed Him to the Throne, and ever since, the stream of unceasing adoration has proclaimed that—to His Church— He is both Lord and God.

In his address on the day of Pentecost, Peter testified that the despised Jesus had been exalted to sit at God's right hand, and he brought his message to its climax with the words: "Therefore let all the house of Israel know assuredly, that God hath made that same Jesus, whom ye have crucified, both Lord and Christ" (Acts 2:36).

Announced as Lord and Christ by the angel at His birth, the lowly Saviour had been such in Person amid every scene of rejection. But except for the devotion of the few who loved Him, He had been accorded nothing of the dignity and homage due to Him. Now all the dishonour was past. God answered the taunt of the chief priests: "Let Him deliver Him now, if He will have Him" (Mt. 27:43) by raising the Crucified from the dead and lifting Him to the Throne, thereby giving Him befitting honour. By thus attesting the person of the Man of Calvary, and by giving Him all the glory attendant upon these His rightful titles, God made Him both Lord and Christ.

Among the functions of majesty attaching to the Lord Jesus in His heavenly enthronement, there may be especially noted these three: the sending forth of the Holy Spirit, the headship of the Church, and the stewardship of the household of God. Before He was crucified, He told His disciples that He would send to them from the Father the Comforter, the Spirit of truth. In the resurrection, the promise was reiterated in His words: "Ye shall be baptized with the Holy Ghost not many days hence" (Acts 1:5). Fulfillment was given on the day of Pentecost, and Peter urged its fact as undeniable proof that Christ had reached the Throne. "Therefore being by the right hand of God exalted, and having received of the Father the promise of the Holy Ghost, He hath shed forth this, which ye now see and hear" (Acts 2:33).

Nothing could witness more eloquently to the place given to the glorified Jesus than this, that still displaying the memorials of His humiliation in His nail-printed body, He should send forth a veritable Person of the eternal Godhead to indwell His believing ones on earth. Speaking not from Himself, but whatever He should hear, and that surely from the enthroned Son, the Holy Spirit would minister the things of Christ, and in all things glorify Him.

The immediate result of the coming of the Spirit was the incorporation of the believers into a body of which the heavenly Christ was Head, into a church of which He was Lord. Not till He was seated far above all was Christ given as "Head over all things" to the church.

His headship involved three factors: primacy, supremacy, and adequacy. In the first, He was His church's source; in the second, its sovereign; and in the third, its supply. All through the centuries since the Spirit came, there has been displayed the wonder of a heavenly church sojourning on an earth from which it has derived nothing pertaining to its true character. Its only source has been its unseen Head. The only law current through the whole of its world-wide dimension has been the will of the Lord whose glory no scornful eye has beheld. The secret of its continuance amid loneliness, peril, and temptation, has been the never-failing ministry of its Head by His Spirit, whereby every need has been met. How wonderful that His body has received everything from One beyond both the sight and reach of the unbelieving world.

Finally, Christ is God's steward. In a striking passage in Isaiah 22, we read of one Eliakim, whom God called His servant. To him was promised the dignity of robe, girdle, and government. The key of the house of David was to be on his shoulder, so that he should open, and none should shut; and he should shut, and none should open. He was to be fastened as a nail in a sure place, so that upon him every vessel should be safely hung. The language of this passage is taken up in the description of the glory of Christ as seen by John in Patmos. The apostle beheld Him invested with the garment and girdle, and heard Him say: "These things saith He that is holy, He that is true, He that hath the key of David, He that openeth, and no man shutteth; and shutteth and no man openeth...behold, I have set before thee an open door, and no man can shut it" (Rev. 3:7-8).

The steward of the ancient house controlled all the wealth of his master, and supervised all his servants. Our exalted Master, who once for our sakes became poor, is now the treasurer of the resources of the infinite God. Indeed He is both treasury and treasure. In the morning of their day, He sends forth His servants equipped for their toil. Through all its hours He appoints their work, and over-rules with almighty power so that none can hinder or defy Him. When the day is past, He shall appraise all their service, and give His rewards. Amid all the unrest and turmoil of this present world, He is the strength and stay of His people, so that all their service, whether great or small, rests securely on Him. Nothing that is of Himself is lost as trivial, but shall remain when heaven and earth pass away. This authority given to our beloved Lord embraces in its scope both heaven and earth. It shall never cease, and when He comes, His servants shall find that their labour is not in vain in the Lord.

"We see Jesus...crowned with glory and honour" (Heb. 2:9). This is all our need. Let us rejoice in the vision glorious, and with pilgrim steps follow the Captain of our salvation to the Land where He has gone.

> *King of Glory, Thou hast triumphed,*
> *Mighty in the battle Thou;*
> *Everlasting doors uplifted,*
> *Welcome Thee as Victor now.*
> *Principalities and powers*
> *Spoiled by Thee, most holy Lord,*
> *Far above them Thou are seated,*
> *On the very Throne of God.*
>
> *At His side whom Thou didst honour,*
> *Glorify on earth the name,*
> *Finish all the work He gave Thee,*
> *All the boundless Love proclaim—*
> *At His side in cloudless splendour,*
> *Till Thou for Thy bride shalt come,*
> *And amid Thy longed-for glory,*
> *Take her to Thy Father's home.*
>
> *Lo, in resurrection glory,*
> *Thou art throned in heaven above,*
> *Where Thou dwellest in the fulness*
> *Of the Father's changeless love—*
> *Love bestowed on Thee unmeasured,*
> *Ere the heavens were begun,*
> *Love of God the everlasting,*
> *To His everlasting Son.*

And the Father, Thee beholding,
Sees the Son that pleased Him well,
Undefiled, and ever holy,
Though 'midst sinners Thou didst dwell.
From that life on earth there rises
To the Father on His Throne,
Incense sweet of rare perfection,
Making all Thy glories known.

All Thy garments smell of aloes,
Perfect Thou each weary hour;
All Thy garments smell of cassia,
Token of the Spirit's power;
Myrrh their texture fills with fragrance,
Symbol of Thy suffering—
Lamb of God, as we behold Thee,
Adoration would we bring.

Now to ages of the ages,
Crowned with honour Thou shalt be;
All the heavenly hosts unceasing,
Glory, might, ascribe to Thee.
Fadeless this Thy royal splendour,
Purchased by Thy precious blood;
Thine the praise of every creature,
Holy Son and Christ of God.

—H. C. H.

CHAPTER ELEVEN

His Priesthood

Peace, peace is mine! On high is Christ appearing,
Within the veil my great High Priest is He;
Honour and glory as a crown He's wearing,
Who wore on earth the crown of thorns for me.
—D. Russele

When the Lord Jesus passed within the veil at His ascension, He entered on the exercise of a priesthood as unique in its glory as it is in its sphere. Earth had known priests who, according to their capacity, had sought to approach God on behalf of their fellowmen. Some had stood for brief moments in His presence and then retired in reverent fear from that dread sanctity. As befitted their ritual, they had drawn near to Him with the blood of sacrifice, but it was blood that could never take away sins. One by one they had relinquished their ministry through mortal weakness, and passed to others the brief dignity of their ceremonial access to God. Then from the land where types and shadows had so long filled men's gaze, the risen Christ arrived to begin His priesthood in the heaven of heavens. Never had a priest been known in that august place, nor had intercession been made before by One radiant with the majesty of the everlasting Throne.

For the child of God in his daily life, no glimpse of Christ's heavenly glory is more urgent than that which shows Him as the Great High Priest. Until his race is run, the believer is tried with distress without and within. He is made to bear the pressure of many a care in a restless, changing world, and to be increasingly conscious of his own frailty. In such circumstances, he is cast on the One whose work can never fail, to find that all his need for succour and for strength is met by the ministry that goes on unceasingly within the veil.

Not only in regard to the believer's path of weakness, but in respect to his own privilege of access in spirit to the holiest, he is entirely dependent on the High Priest. In that realm of light he would be all alone were it not for the blessed presence of the Head of the priestly house, in whom he is accepted, and who, for His people's sake, wears the golden crown of glory and honour.

What we consider in this chapter is not so much our Lord's priestly ministry, wonderful though it is, but His priestly glory. The latter is the key to the former. Christ possesses everything requisite for His exalted service. Nothing is lacking to His personal fitness for every exercise of His priesthood. In the glowing chapters of the Epistle to the Hebrews, He is revealed to us as Priest in a sevenfold dignity whereby He is "perfected for evermore" (Heb. 7:28, marg.). Note in succession these seven aspects of His fulness:

His Resources of Deity: In the first chapter of the epistle, we hear the Father address His Beloved in resurrection with the words of joyous greeting: "Thou art My Son, this day have I begotten Thee" (Heb. 1:5). That the words refer to the resurrection, and that this Sonship is the very basis of His priesthood, are both clearly shown in the statement of chapter 5: "Christ glorified not Himself to be made an High Priest but He that said unto Him, Thou art My Son, today have I begotten Thee" (v. 5). Whenever the source of priesthood is described to us in Scripture, it is always a matter of sonship. Aaron's dignity was related to his descent from Levi, for the latter's tribe was taken as the firstborn (Num. 3:12), and given the Thummim and Urim (Deut. 33:8). The believer priests of the New Testament order are such by virtue of their spiritual birth, and are addressed in Hebrews as holy brethren.

To His present ministry the Lord brings the resources of His eternal Person. He understands fully every claim of the character of God before whom He represents us. His intercession is bound by no limitations either of knowledge or of wisdom, such as mark the petitions that rise from our hearts. Never will His work for us fall short of that which will satisfy God. No one less than Himself in the greatness of His being could deal with all the weight of our care. Myriads of prayers ascend from His people on earth during even one day. In every land they tell Him of their need, and cast themselves on His grace, but He is never distracted by the multiplicity of requests, nor does He miss one single cry. He is not wearied with the burden, nor made to defer for a moment the consideration of our case.

It is His Sonship that is brought before us in the Word as being a ground of confident assurance that He will be faithful to us in all His ministry. Moses was faithful as a servant, but Christ is faithful as a Son over God's house (Heb. 3:6, R.V. marg.). The Son not only loves the house, but loves the Father, and will always guard the Father's honour in the house. Two aspects of truth are thus linked inseparably. Christ is the Son over the house, yet we have an high priest over the house of God (Heb. 10:21). "Seeing then that we have a great High Priest, that is passed into the heavens, Jesus the Son of God, let us hold fast our profession" (Heb. 4:14).

His Experience in Suffering Humanity: Our Lord walked in this scene in the fulness of Godhead, but it was "Godhead incarnate in weakness and pain."

"Forasmuch then as the children are partakers of flesh

and blood, He also Himself likewise took part of the same"
(Heb. 2:14). In His possession of true Manhood, He tasted
deeply of the trials that afflict His people. Far from being a
stranger to weariness, loneliness, and anguish, He was "a
Man of sorrows, and acquainted with grief." There is no
valley in which He leads His saints which has not first
been traversed by His own feet. We read that "He Himself
hath suffered being tempted" (Heb. 2:18), and that He
"endured such contradiction of sinners against Himself"
(Heb. 12:3).

Again it is written that "though He were a Son, yet
learned He obedience by the things which He suffered"
(Heb. 5:8). It was not that He learned how to obey; this He
always knew. We in our sinfulness must be taught this by
the subduing of our will, by bringing into captivity every
thought to the obedience of Christ. That which the Holy
One learned in suffering—His own obedience—was the
practical cost of doing the will of God in a godless world.

When Scripture says that the Captain of our salvation
was made perfect through sufferings (Heb. 2:10), the reference is not to His character but to His completeness of
qualification for His present ministry. His character was
always beautiful in holiness. In its absolute perfection, it
was capable neither of change nor of addition to its traits.
His sufferings gave Him that fulness of experience out of
which He now has compassion for us in our weakness. "For
we have not an High Priest which cannot be touched with
the feeling of our infirmities; but was in all points tempted
like as we are, yet without sin" (Heb. 4:15).

Being made "like unto His brethren," He is "a merciful
and faithful High Priest" (Heb. 2:17), merciful in the tender
sympathy of His heart, and faithful in its outflow of intercession and grace. It was therefore most fitting, and indeed
becoming to God Himself that Christ should go to His

priesthood by the path of suffering that His people tread.

His Divine Appointment: It is God's prerogative to determine who shall approach Him, and who therefore shall deal with Him on behalf of others, if necessary making offerings for their sake. Jeroboam made priests of the lowest of the people, which were not of the sons of Levi, but it was all of his own devising, and invited the sure judgment of God. Apart from all such spurious pretensions, it is true that "no man taketh this honour unto himself, but he that is called of God, as was Aaron" (Heb. 5:4). The world is full of the exaltation of self, but nothing of this dark pride had any place in the heart and ways of the lowly Saviour. "Christ glorified not Himself to be made an High Priest" (Heb. 5:5). His entry into His heavenly ministry was altogether of God, who delighted in Him, and it witnessed that He was all that God's heart could desire. Hence His divine appointment betokened the reality of the divine satisfaction.

The deep pleasure in His Son in which God exalted Him to the Throne was seen in prophetic light a thousand years before the ascension. David by the Spirit of God looked across the centuries, heard the Lord say to his Lord: "Sit Thou on My right hand," and bore thrilling testimony to that mighty induction to heavenly majesty. "The Lord hath sworn, and will not repent, Thou art a Priest forever after the order of Melchizedek" (Ps. 110:1-5). So significant are David's words that they are expressly quoted three times in the Hebrews Epistle (5:6; 7:17, 21), and three times referred to in part (5:10; 6:20; 7:11). Not only was the Son given the salute of solemn dignity (named of God a High Priest, 5:10, R.V.), but the appointment was confirmed by oath: "The Lord hath sworn, and will not repent." When God made promise to Abraham, He added His oath to His promise, that to Abraham and all the heirs of promise there might be given two immutable things in which it was impossible for Him to lie, i.e., His promise and His oath. The sons of Levi knew nothing of the honour of appointment by oath to their priesthood; it was reserved for the One whose glory should infinitely transcend theirs. They were frail mortals; He was the Son risen in power.

His Perpetuity in Resurrection: So glorious is the priesthood of Christ that the Aaronic model could not be an adequate picture of it. It pleased the Author of Scripture in His perfect wisdom to liken another man to the Son in respect to this matter. Melchizedek was made like Christ, but not Christ to Melchizedek. The likeness was derived partly from what was revealed concerning him in Scripture, and partly from the fact that much was hidden. That which was revealed showed Melchizedek to be a type of Christ in the two aspects of royalty and of worth of character, for he was "King of righteousness," and "King of peace" (Heb. 7:2).

In that much was hidden, namely, all record of his ancestry, his birth, and his death, he was displayed on the page of Scripture (and in that sense alone) as an abiding priest unrelated to any prior ministrant. Thus he typified Christ in the two further aspects of solitariness and permanency. To seek to link his identity with that of any worthy of the past is futile, for obviously to identify Melchizedek is to mar the type.

Christ's royalty still awaits its display, but His character was vindicated by His resurrection. His priesthood is indeed a solitary one, derived from God's appraisal of the surpassing excellence of His Person and of His atoning work. Its permanency partakes of eternity; He is a Priest forever. Three functions are linked with His priesthood: offering, intercession, and blessing. Of these the first was complete in His Cross, and the second shall be finished when all need for it is past, but the third shall never cease.

Of this last it may be observed that the attitude in which the Lord took leave of His disciples at Olivet, that of lifting up His hands in blessing on them, indicated the eternal ministry to which He went. When every sadness of our journey and every trace of our frailty are gone, and we shine in the fulness of our salvation, then those priestly hands will still lavish on us the exceeding riches of the divine grace. The sight of them will fill each heart with solemn gladness, for while the hands of both Melchizedek and Aaron were uplifted in blessing, they were never pierced hands.

It is by virtue of His resurrection that Christ possesses an abiding priesthood, for He "is made, not after the law of a carnal commandment, but after the power of an endless life" (Heb. 7:16). Only as risen from the dead could He be Priest. His appointment was not like that priesthood which took up mortal men until such time as they laid down their office in death.

On the contrary, His appointment was based on the entire fitness of His indissoluble life to be the sphere of His ministry, a ministry glorious in the outpouring of its might. Aaron must give place to Eleazar, and the latter to Phinehas; the Son of God will need no successor. "This Man, because He continueth ever hath an unchangeable priesthood. Wherefore He is able also to save them to the uttermost that come unto God by Him, seeing He ever liveth to make intercession for them" (Heb. 7:24-25). Neither His prayer nor its sequence in the salvation of His people in every need they have along their journey shall be interrupted by any weakness on His part, nor shall any change pass over His feelings towards them, nor will His desire wane from seeking their perfect good.

His Moral Glory: "For such a High Priest became us, holy, guileless, undefiled, separated from sinners, and made higher than the heavens" (Heb. 7:26, R.V.). He is, and ever has been, intrinsically holy. There was in Him no sin to disturb the purity of His heart as He walked this earth, nor can such be in His present majesty. In His relation to men He is guileless, seeking not their hurt but only their salvation, even as in the contemptible treatment of His rejection no guile was found in His mouth. He is undefiled in respect of all the corruption that marks our poor race. No touch of evil marred the beauty of His ways as He walked in a world of sin, nor can it attach to Him within the holiest above.

The priests of the order of Aaron needed the constant washings of their ritual; our Priest who ministers is immaculate in His heart and ways. He is thus separated from sinners by the wonder of His character in life, in death, and in His ascension. There is such a gulf between His moral excellence and the sinfulness of men (i.e., of priests and people alike in the ancient order) that His priesthood is utterly unique. Moreover, all is attested by the fact that He is made higher than the heavens, that He has been received to God's throne as entirely worthy of His place there.

Much of the Epistle to the Hebrews has for its background the ritual of the day of atonement in Israel, and lessons are taught by comparison and contrast. Among the features peculiar to that day was the entrance of the high priest within the veil. It is to be noted that during those crucial hours he went in more than once into the holiest.

First of all, he took a censer full of burning coals of fire off the altar before the Lord, and with his hands full of sweet incense beaten small, he brought it within the veil. He put the incense on the fire before the Lord, that the cloud of the incense might cover the mercy seat on the testimony. This, we read, was done that he die not (see Lev. 16:12-13). Not till the cloud of incense rose could he dare present the blood of sacrifice by sprinkling it on and before the mercy seat. Had he gone in with blood apart from incense, he would have died.

Considering the lessons of this ritual, and beholding the uniqueness of Christ's entry into heaven, we see that the fragrant incense speaks of the beauty of holiness which was our Lord's personal ground of entrance. It was in His own holiness that He endured death; it was in the same holiness that He went within the veil. Had He not possessed such glory of character, He could have been neither Sacrifice nor Priest. He needed no blood from a sacrifice as His own title to heaven. But He was pleased to enter not only by right of character but by right of the sacrifice of Himself in order that we who had no right to enter might do so on the ground of that same sacrifice and the shedding of His own precious blood.

His All-Sufficient Sacrifice: "Such an High Priest…who needeth not daily, as those high priests, to offer up sacrifices, first for his own sins, and then for the people's: for this He did once, when He offered up Himself" (Heb. 7:26-27). "For every high priest is ordained to offer gifts and sacrifices: wherefore it is of necessity that this Man have somewhat also to offer" (Heb. 8:3). The primary responsibility of the priest was that of offering to God the gifts and sacrifices which He approved.

In the case of the high priests of the Aaronic order, two things were evident. First, they were required to offer for their own sins. Secondly, such sacrifices as they offered, whether for their sins or those of the people, had to be repeated regularly throughout their ministry. The priesthood of Christ is in glorious contrast with a dignity all of its own. On the one hand, He needed not to offer for Himself, for He had no sins. On the other hand, His offering for His people's sins required no repetition, but dealt with them once for all. Thus we read that "every priest standeth daily ministering and offering oftentimes the same sacrifices, which can never take away sins; but this Man, after He had offered one sacrifice for sins forever, sat down on the right hand of God" (Heb. 10:11-12).

It was not that Christ was a Priest at the Cross; there He was the Offerer. But now all the worth of that completed offering attaches to Him as Priest. When He went within the veil at His ascension, He was accepted as the One whose sacrifice at Calvary was of such infinite value that there could be no addition. This acceptance declared that all His priestly obligation to provide an offering for sins was completely fulfilled. In this sense, He was an "High Priest in things pertaining to God, to make reconciliation [lit., to propitiate] for the sins of the people" (Heb. 2:17).

This obligation being met forever, He continues now the work of intercession and blessing, not regarding the sins of His people, but their infirmities. His present priestly ministry therefore rests on the abiding significance of its profound inaugurative act—His entry within the veil—and that in turn rests on the finished work of the Cross.

Adoringly we look up to the Throne and see the record of that all-sufficient sacrifice written in the hands and feet and side of our High Priest. We hear Him saying to us, as in the prophecy to Zion: "I have graven thee upon the palms of My hands" (see Isa. 49:16). His own Person bears the witness to the finished work of atonement.

> *...His own wounds in heaven declare*
> *His work on earth is done.*

There, too, is the assurance that He is merciful and faithful, that He can never forget us, and that all our needs may be entrusted safely to Him.

His Heavenly Enthronement: "We have such an High

Priest, who is set on the right hand of the throne of the Majesty in the heavens; a minister of the sanctuary, and of the true tabernacle, which the Lord pitched, and not man" (Heb. 8:1-2). "Christ is not entered into the holy places made with hands, which are the figures of the true; but into heaven itself, now to appear in the presence of God for us" (Heb. 9:24). It must have been with great awe that Israel waited while Aaron went into the tabernacle on the first Day of Atonement, and while he approached the mercy seat for the brief moments of his service there. It must have been also with great fear that Aaron entered the august presence of his God.

Nevertheless, the Presence graciously dwelt in a temporary structure made by men from material things. The value of these materials lay not in themselves but in that which they typified, glories yet to be made known. Aaron's ceremonial entry was utterly eclipsed by the reality of the entry of Christ. Our Lord Jesus is Priest, not of the material and the transient, but of the spiritual and the eternal; not of the earthly and human, but of the heavenly and divine.

The Holiest into which Aaron went was indeed the place of the divine government, but it could never offer a throne to him or even to Moses, the mediator, who there received the revelation of the mind of God. As befitting his position as a creature, and because his service had no completeness in itself, bringing no abiding rest, Aaron stood in the presence of God.

Christ, however, is set on the right hand of the Throne. His work of offering is forever finished, and from it not only the hearts of His people are satisfied, but God Himself has received the savour of eternal rest. There our Lord Jesus Christ sits at God's right hand. By changeless right the Throne is His, and He administers its bounty in an unceasing supply of mercy and grace to those who still make their pilgrim way on earth. Because He is there, they draw near in spirit, marked by reverent boldness to receive from Him that all-sufficient supply. Therefore they sing in triumph and in trust:

> *Peace! perfect peace!—our future all unknown;*
> *Jesus we know, and He is on the Throne.*

CHAPTER TWELVE

The Lamb

The Lamb is all the glory
Of Immanuel's land.
— Anne Ross Cousin

It is a remarkable fact that in the New Testament the title "Lamb" is seldom used of the Lord Jesus prior to the pages of the Revelation. In the Gospels it occurs only twice, and that in one chapter (Jn. 1:29, 36). There the Baptist, as the one in whom all the ancient line of witness to Christ reached its climax, gathered up all the sacrificial association of the word and proclaimed his Lord as "the Lamb of God which taketh away the sin of the world." Then again beholding the walk so marked by purity and gentleness, gave voice to his thoughts in earnest tribute: "Behold the Lamb of God."

In the Acts, Christ is spoken of as the Lamb only in the quotation from Isaiah 53 read by the Ethiopian eunuch (Acts 8:32). In the Epistles, the term is used only once, and that in reference to His perfection as the sinless Sacrifice (1 Pet. 1:19). In the Revelation, however, it acquires a peculiar glory, being used twenty-eight times, and always in circumstances of supreme majesty.

As the Lamb, Christ was the rejected One, slain in unresisting meekness. Therefore it is as the Lamb that He will be invested with universal rule, will know the joy of His marriage feast, will triumph over all His foes, and will reign forever and ever. Men despised the beauty of His character; they must learn God's appreciation of it. Earth saw Him laden with dark dishonour and nailed to the shameful Cross; it must see Him on His throne of glory and weighted with eternal triumphs.

This answer of God's honour to man's reproach has its effect increased by the fact that in every instance in the Revelation it is a diminutive form of the word "lamb" that is used. How little He was in the eyes of His scorners, and how little they thought that the destiny of the universe rested in those pierced hands, that a dying Man—the theme alike of priestly jest and of drunken song—would assume such sovereignty that of the increase of His government and peace there should be no end!

Taken into heaven in his vision of the future, John sees the eternal Throne, and in the right hand of Him that sits on it a seven-sealed book, the title deeds of earthly dominion. We forget that in spite of the deeds of the usurper the authority symbolized in this book has always been in God's hand. No turbulence of evil has progressed one hair's breadth beyond the limit set by His permissive will.

Moreover, John learns that the possession of this dominion and the execution of its judgment wait for One who shall be worthy of them. Many have desired this honour; only One is worthy.

Then, in the midst of the Throne, "in the heart of its blaze," the apostle sees standing "a Lamb as it had been slain, having seven horns and seven eyes, which are the seven Spirits of God sent forth into all the earth" (Rev. 5:6). The vision is that of the Lord Jesus Christ, still bearing in His glorified body the marks of His death, yet displaying the splendour of omnipotence (seven horns), and of omniscience (seven eyes), and of omnipresence (seven Spirits sent forth into all the earth). He is acclaimed as the Lion of Judah, the leader of the armies of God, and as the Root of David—David's Son and David's Lord. The Lion is, nevertheless, the Lamb; in the mystery of His Person the majesty of Deity shines from the beauty of humanity.

The Lamb is King by right and King by conquest. In His humiliation in death, He prevailed that He might open the book, and so John sees Him take it from God's hand, in readiness to loose the seals and enter into its promise. Once in the synagogue of Nazareth, He closed the book of the prophecy, before the words "the day of vengeance of our God" (see Lk. 4:30). Now, in the vision, the time for vengeance is come, and the Lamb must be its executor.

But before the seals are touched, and the process of judgment is set in motion, the Lamb is seen surrounded by three circles of adoration, different in their character, yet all concentric to Him. To Him they ascribe all worthiness, but it is to Him as the Lamb. Thus His sacrifice and His royalty are forever blended in their praise. Nearest to Him are His redeemed ones, previously raptured to heaven at His coming for His saints (Jn. 14:3; 1 Thess. 4:16-17), and now resplendent in the twofold honour of priestly maturity (i.e., as elders) and of administrative function (i.e., as living creatures). To Him they bow to present their homage as His heavenly nobility, and to Him they sing their new song— new on their lips, and new in heaven's courts.

Around them are the myriads of the angelic hosts. With what awe and wonder must these have considered their Lord's path of lowliness and love! They saw Him in infant form in the manger, bowed in sorrow in the garden, dying on the Cross, and silent in the tomb. Now they behold His investiture with His earthly sovereignty, and they raise their voice to give Him their sevenfold praise.

Finally, as if it reverberated through the open door of heaven from the kingdom soon-to-be, John hears the tribute of the creation that once groaned and travailed in pain together, but at last rejoices in being delivered from the

bondage of corruption into the glorious liberty of the children of God (Rom. 8:21-22). "Worthy is the Lamb!"

Amid the scenes of glory and judgment which throng the
Revelation is one which, though not in the sequence which
portrays His triumph as the Lamb, is nevertheless so rich in
its unfolding of the Person of Christ that we must notice it
here. In chapter 10, an angel appears robed in the splendour that belongs only to the throne of God. The setting
shows us the plagues that follow the sounding of the trum-
pets, plagues reminiscent of those of ancient Egypt—
falling upon idolaters, as they fell in that day, but far
exceeding them in their nature and intensity.

As the visitation upon Egypt culminated in the deliverance of Israel by the Angel of the cloud, so for Israel's sake
there appears the same glorious Person, and once more, as
related to Israel, in angelic guise. Though no titles of
majesty are used of Him in this scene, the identity of the
Angel is beyond mistake. He is clothed with the cloud so
often associated with His presence, and on His head is the
rainbow that otherwise encircles the Throne. This is the
pledge of His abiding faithfulness, however dark may be
the storm that bursts on His ancient people. The bow with
its emerald brightness prefigures the summer of resurrection after the winter of Israel's national death. The Angel's
face is as the sun, for He is the Sun of Righteousness, the
true sun to rule the Day of the Kingdom. Government
springs not from the will of the people, but from God, and
it must ultimately be exercised by this glorious One. His
feet are as pillars of fire; with unfaltering tread and with
burning holiness He marches to His kingdom.

Setting His right foot on the sea, and His left foot on the
earth, the Angel claims both for Himself. As the promise
was to Joshua that every place should be his whereon the
sole of his foot should tread, so it belongs to the greater

than Joshua, even to Him whom Joshua worshipped as the Captain of the host of the Lord. Every part of this globe must be His.

Jesus shall reign where'er the sun
Doth His successive journeys run.

With a loud voice as when a lion roars, this Lion of Judah asserts His right to take vengeance on His enemies, and to take the kingdom to Himself. In majestic reply, the seven thunders utter their voices. When the Son of God, as He neared the Cross, spoke of His hour of anguish, and prayed: "Father, glorify Thy name," the Father answered, "I have both glorified it, and will glorify it again." But the people standing by said that it thundered (Jn. 12:28-29). Here in Revelation 10, the same voice speaks, and gives sevenfold response to the claim of the Angel. Then with uplifted hand the Angel takes solemn oath by the living God, the Creator, that the mystery of God shall be finished. This mystery, this constant problem of God's ways in permitting sin, suffering, and sorrow, this enigma from whose shadow no life is exempt, shall be finished, consummated in the achievement of all its secret purpose by the revelation of the King in His beauty, and by the display of the blessings of His reign.

Returning to the glimpses of the Lamb in heaven, we pass on to the exceeding joy of Revelation 19. John hears, "as it were the voice of a great multitude, and as the voice of many waters, and as the voice of mighty thunderings, saying, Alleluia; for the Lord God omnipotent reigneth. Let us be glad and rejoice, and give honour to Him: for the marriage of the Lamb is come, and His wife hath made herself ready" (Rev. 19:6-7). Like the strains of some great wedding march, four Allelujas peal forth in sublime prelude to "the Lamb's great bridal feast of bliss and love."

It has been a long time since the Baptist summed up the witness to the sufferings of Christ in his words: "Behold the Lamb," and to the glory of Christ in those other words: "He that hath the bride is the bridegroom" (Jn. 1:29; 3:29). It waits for the voice of celestial throngs to bring both suffering and glory together in one brief yet profound phrase: "The marriage of the Lamb." Did language at any time convey so much in so few words? The marriage is the Lamb's. His was the purchase price by which He obtained the Bride. His alone is the worthiness for such surpassing joy.

Our souls will vibrate to the music of the heavenly praise as among His redeemed we gaze on our Bridegroom's face. Its threefold burden will be that God reigns, that all heaven is filled with rejoicing, and that Christ is satisfied. We recall the words of the prophet: "He shall see of the travail of His soul, and shall be satisfied" (Isa. 53:11). Were it not for the express language of Scripture, we might wonder what could give Him such joy that He would count it adequate recompense for the sufferings of the Cross. "The pleasure of the Lord shall prosper in His hand" (Isa. 53:10). Every sequence of His sorrow shall add its share to His satisfaction. Indeed, the bliss of His marriage is only part of the Lamb's recompense. Calvary's woe shall find its outcome not only in the wedding feast, but in the triumph of the millennial reign and in all the ineffable vistas of the glory of eternity.

Immediately following this festal joy is the victory of the Lamb over His enemies. John says concerning the legions that follow earth's last tyrant in his mad defiance of heaven's authority: "These shall make war with the Lamb, and the Lamb shall overcome them; for He is Lord of lords, and King of kings" (Rev. 17:14). As the Lord Jesus descends to vanquish His foes, He finds earth a scene of chaos and misery, but our eyes do not rest on this. Rather, we behold His many glories, and rejoice that the misrule of the centuries gives place to His righteous and peaceful reign. Heaven is opened, and from it comes the King of glory riding prosperously in His majesty because of truth and meekness and righteousness (see Ps. 45:4). He comes faithful to fulfill His every promise.

He judges and makes war. His eyes are as a flame of fire; nothing escapes the scrutiny of His holiness; no sham of earth avoids detection. Upon His head are many diadems; every title of royalty is His throughout the earth; He alone has strength to sustain their burden. He has a name written that no man knows but He Himself. It is His own "…secret name of undisclosed delight." It indicates the glory of an exclusive relationship with God, and shows that the sweetness of His heart's joy, and the bitterness of the suffering to which it gives answer, are alike beyond the capacity of the creature to comprehend (Rev. 19:11-12).

"His name is called the Word of God" (Rev. 19:13). Once He was manifested in grace as the Word of Life. He was heard, was seen by human eyes, looked upon, and handled by human hands (1 Jn. 1:1). Now in judgment He is the Word of God, whose coming is the final setting forth of God's mind touching earth's rebellion, and who is Himself all God's revelation touching earth's kingship. His advent in glory brings doom on the proud leaders of this world.

The battle rages, but One alone takes part in the conflict when the armies from heaven meet the armies of earth. The Lamb displays His wrath, and the wicked are slain with the breath of His lips (Isa. 11:4). The time has come when the King fulfills His word through Moses: "If I whet My glittering sword, and My hand take hold on judgment; I will render vengeance to Mine enemies, and will reward them that hate Me" (Deut. 32:41). It is the day wherein the Lord

alone is exalted (Isa. 2:11). He takes His kingly throne and
the government is upon His shoulder (Isa. 9:6).

John sees the Lamb stand on Mount Sion (Rev. 14:1).
This the Father decreed: "Yet have I set My King upon My
holy hill" (Ps. 2:6). A greater than Solomon sits upon the
throne of His father David, and indeed on the throne of the
Lord (Lk. 1:32; 1 Chron. 29:23). Mount Sion is the city of
the great King (Ps. 48:2). The moon is confounded, and the
sun ashamed, for the Lord of hosts reigns in Sion and in
Jerusalem, and before His ancients gloriously (Isa. 24:23).
The true King of glory rules, the Lord strong and mighty,
the Lord of hosts; the earth is His, and the fulness thereof
(Ps. 24:1, 8-10). He is King over all the earth (Zech. 14:9).
Earth's oppression and cruelty are gone, and the cry of its
sorrow is forever stilled. This One, over whose Cross were
inscribed the words: "This is Jesus the King of the Jews"
(Mt. 27:37), now reigns in righteousness and peace.

It is of this time that the Scripture speaks: "And again
when He bringeth the first-begotten into the world, He
saith, And let all the angels of God worship Him" (Heb.
1:6, marg.). Earth that saw the true Heir of God despised
and cast out now sees Him receive His inheritance. Her
inhabitants behold the angels of God in all their hosts
bowed in adoration before His pierced feet. Now is fulfilled the promise to Nathaniel: "Hereafter ye shall see
heaven open, and the angels of God ascending and
descending upon the Son of man" (Jn. 1:51). Visible at last
to men (see Lk. 9:26; 2 Thess. 1:7), the angels are seen to
do His bidding whose will links both heaven and earth.
Earth itself lies at rest, serene under the smile of an open
heaven, and is "filled with the knowledge of the glory of
the Lord, as the waters cover the sea" (Hab. 2:14).

Passing on through the Revelation to the vision of the
Holy City, we find certain precious glimpses of the Lamb

that take us beyond the bounds of time into eternity. In the symbol of a radiant city we are shown the bride, the Lamb's wife. In every aspect, the city displays the glory of Christ, for Christ-likeness is the dominant feature of the redeemed in their heavenly state. Not only do the excellencies of Christ shine in His glorified people, but in their midst He Himself, "In His beauty, without a veil is seen."

No part of the city is more holy than another. In fact, its presentation in the shape of a cube (Rev. 21:16) reminds us of the Holy of holies in the tabernacle and temple of old. John sees no temple there, but "the Lord God Almighty and the Lamb are the temple of it" (Rev. 21:22). David desired to dwell in the house of the Lord all the days of his life, to behold the beauty of the Lord, and to enquire in His temple (Ps. 27:4). But in this city, the redeemed have God and the Lamb for their enquiry place, gazing on the divine beauty in its undimmed display. Here is direct and unhindered access to God Himself, an open vision of His uncreated majesty.

As there is such manifestation of Deity, it follows that the city has "no need of the sun, neither of the moon, to shine in it: for the glory of God lightens it, and the Lamb is the light thereof" (Rev. 21:23). No created thing is required as a channel for God's gifts to His people. No longer does He use means for the blessing of His beloved ones, but shines on them Himself and directly supplies every element of their eternal bliss.

Nevertheless, the Lamb is the light thereof, so that the radiance that illuminates the city—the glory of God in all its fulness—streams from the blessed Person of God's Christ. If in His humiliation on earth He could say: "He that hath seen Me hath seen the Father," it is surely nonetheless true in the splendour of eternity. There is neither revelation of God nor unveiling of His brightness except in the One whom men rejected, the Son who is Himself the brightness of His glory.

When in that city where is the throne of God and of the Lamb, His servants will serve Him, and they will see His face (Rev. 22:3-4). In their pilgrimage through the world, they have carried in the earthen vessels of their mortal bodies the treasure of "the light of the knowledge of the glory of God in the face of Jesus Christ" (2 Cor. 4:6). In the Holy City they will behold the glory itself, but still displayed on that same face that once was buffeted by sinful hands, that face whose sorrow is past and whose joy now knows no measure. Shall we not pause in worship, and acknowledge to each one: "I've seen the face of Jesus; I can but kiss His feet."

The throne of eternity is the throne of God and of the Lamb. As the Lamb, Christ was rejected and slain; as the Lamb He reigns unceasingly. Even of His servants it is said that they reign for ever and ever; how much more must it be true of Him! The witness of Scripture allows no doubt in this matter. "Unto the Son He saith, Thy throne, O God, is for ever and ever" (Heb. 1:8). Again, it speaks of "the everlasting kingdom of our Lord and Saviour Jesus Christ" (2 Pet. 1:11).

Nor is it taught otherwise in the words of 1 Corinthians 15:24-28, "Then cometh the end, when He shall have delivered up the kingdom to God, even the Father; when He shall have put down all rule and all authority and power. For He must reign, till He hath put all enemies under His feet...and when all things shall be subdued unto Him, then shall the Son also Himself be subject unto Him that put all things under Him, that God may be all in all."

The parallelism of verse 24 indicates the burden of the passage. The "delivering up" finds its counterpart in the "putting down" of all opposition. It is not that Christ ceases to reign, but that He brings all to the Father. Even in the Millennium, the kingdom is the Father's (see Mt. 6:10; 13:43; 26:29), but the rule is by the hands of the Son. The more the foes that are put down, the more truly is the Kingdom the Father's. When every foe is gone, it is all His.

When the grand goal of 1 Corinthians 15:24 is reached, the universe will be in absolute subjection. Even death is destroyed, and the kingdom is the Father's in totality. In the very climax of His victory, the Son manifests His subjection to God, but this He ever did in His path on earth. It is not His subjection that is new in this passage, only its circumstance. Thus all things are subject to the Son, and in His subjection, they are subject to God. God is all in all, no longer sundered from His creatures by their sinfulness and mortality, but in direct and continuous relation to them.

This, then, is no eclipse of the glory of the Son. Rather it is the vindication of His Person in the final achievement of that which He sought in suffering and in death—the honour of the Father's name. Here is the goal to which the Son has borne all things by the word of His power. Throughout the journey it has been true that "in Him all things consist" (Col. 1:17, R.V.). It shall be true forever.

Thus on the throne of God, even when all things shall be delivered to the Father, we see the Lamb. And we shall see Him bearing the marks of His Cross as a perpetual memorial to the foundation of the eternal order—the fulness of His atonement. And the lost, who refused to be loosed from their sins by His precious blood, shall know in their eternal doom that they are controlled by perfect righteousness, and that the Lamb, whose will they must do through compulsion, rules by flawless title and is rightly the Sovereign of the universe.

As we meditate on the unfading glories that adorn His once thorn-crowned brow, we recall the opening words of

His last message through His servant John: "I Jesus have sent Mine angel to testify unto you these things in the churches. I am the root and the offspring of David, and the bright and morning star" (Rev. 22:16). We have mused on the records of His greatness and of His dignity, but following them all is the voice that tells us that He is still the same beloved Saviour whom we have learned to trust and to adore. Instead of greeting us here with a recital of His infinite majesty, and with the mention of the titles of His eternal excellency, He takes the name Jesus, the Saviour-name that was written above Him on the Cross. It is the name that tells of His tender grace and of His dying love. He changes not. The shame of the Tree gives place to the honour of the Throne, but He Himself is the same. We wait for His coming, rejoicing that He has said: "Surely I come quickly." How glad we shall be then, to be forever with the One who is even now the Life of our life.

Even so, come, Lord Jesus.

Scripture Index